Social Capital and the Happiness of Nations

Christian Kroll

Social Capital and the Happiness of Nations

The Importance of Trust and Networks for Life Satisfaction in a Cross-National Perspective

PETER LANG
Frankfurt am Main · Berlin · Bern · Bruxelles · New York · Oxford · Wien

Bibliographic Information published by the Deutsche Nationalbibliothek
The Deutsche Nationalbibliothek lists this publication in the Deutsche Nationalbibliografie; detailed bibliographic data is available in the internet at <http://www.d-nb.de>.

ISBN 978-3-631-57015-9

www.peterlang.de

Für meine Eltern

Contents

Acknowledgements

A number of people contributed their sophisticated ideas and knowledge to this book. I am deeply grateful to Barbara Beham, Sonja Drobnic, Mareike Gronwald, Sarah Knirsch, Oliver Kroll, Anna Müller-Pankkonen, Birgit Pfau-Effinger, Nickie Povel, Braden Roberts and Torben Schulz. Furthermore, this book would not be possible without the remarkable efforts of all the scholars mentioned in it. My gratitude also belongs to the institutions whose data the analyses are based on: the World Bank, World Values Survey Group, Freedom House and UNU-WIDER. Finally, I would like to thank Peter Lang Publishing Group, in particular Andrea Kolb, Kathrin Kummer and Michael Ruecker, for their support.

C.K.

Hamburg, January 2008

Foreword

"All things considered, how satisfied are you with your life as a whole these days?" This single-item question and similar more complex measures have been used worldwide as indicators of subjective well-being (SWB) in social science research, and constitute a vast body of research on subjective indicators of quality of life. Unlike the objective indicators of well-being that focus on available resources and objective living conditions, subjective measures emphasize well-being as experienced and perceived "in the eye of the beholder". In addition to the distinction between objective and subjective indicators, measures can also be classified in terms of level of analysis: a). individual level, b). meso/group level (e.g. family, community), and c). macro (cross-national) level, which is the approach Christian Kroll has chosen in his thesis.

There has been a consistent finding that people in some nations report to be more satisfied with their lives than in other nations. This phenomenon has been linked to economic development of countries; however, other correlates have been explored and found important, such as the level of social capital in a society. Christian Kroll's thesis follows this line of research by examining the effects of social capital on life satisfaction at the aggregate cross-national level.

In his thesis, the author first outlines the state of research on the concepts of life satisfaction and social capital. The SWB is put in context of the broader framework of the quality of life research, so that the reader is provided with useful knowledge of the research field. In the second part of the theoretical background, extensive literature on structural, cognitive and linking social capital is summarized and discussed. This overview provides a firm theoretical and empirical basis for the subsequent hypotheses on the effects of social capital on life satisfaction. The author identifies several mechanisms through which social capital can enhance SWB: a) Memberships and participation in voluntary associations offer the members of a network moral backing and social support that enhance life satisfaction; b) Positive effects of being socially embedded help people to cope with the disadvantages of modernisation; c) Generalized trust brings about low transaction costs and lowers stress, thereby raising SWB; d) Trust in societal institutions prevents people from feeling powerless and helpless; and e) Social capital facilitates economic progress, good health, social cohesion and democracy, all of which are significantly associated with SWB.

In the second part of the thesis, Christian Kroll empirically examines the effects of aggregate level social capital on the mean life satisfaction score in countries for which data were available in the World Values Survey (WVS). The WVS is a unique data base of the values and beliefs of mass publics on political and social life, with more than 80 countries having been covered in four waves in the period 1981-2001. Kroll uses pooled data across several survey waves, and identifies 152 observations for his descriptive and 125 cases for the multivariate regression analysis. Descriptive and bivariate results show considerable differences in national mean satisfaction and indicators of social capital. The relationship between cognitive and structural social capital and life satisfaction is moderate and - as expected - positive. However, when economic indicators are included in the multivariate analysis, the study reveals important differences between rich and poor/middle income countries. Employing the previously suggested threshold of $13.000 GDP per capita, Kroll shows that social capital plays a particularly prominent role in rich countries. Both cognitive social capital (generalized trust) and structural social capital (sum of memberships in different types of voluntary association) are more important determinants of life satisfaction than economic development and other measures of economic performance, including the level of income inequality in a country. In contrast, social capital seems to be considerably less important in developing countries, where economic factors exert a remarkably strong impact on national mean life satisfaction.

Christian Kroll builds on two currently very popular theoretical frameworks: quality of life and social capital. With his comprehensive literature review, he provides a valuable overview of the developments in these fields and convincingly links both research traditions in testable hypotheses on the effects of social capital on life satisfaction. His analysis of pooled WVS data contributes and broadens our understanding of social process as manifested in national satisfaction measures but also opens new questions on measurement issues in cross-national comparative research.

Prof. Sonja Drobnič, PhD
University of Hamburg

1. Introduction

Many people would agree that being "happy" or "satisfied with their lives" is a major goal of their existence. The U.S. Declaration of Independence (1776), for example, considers the "pursuit of happiness" to be one of their citizens' inalienable rights. Likewise, the Constitution of the French Revolution (1793) aspires to enhance "*le bonheur commun*" (Braun 2002: 43) and the government of Buthan today even aims to increase the country's "Gross Happiness Product" (Mulgan 2004). After all, questions about happiness have kept scholars busy for thousands of years now. It is consequently only appropriate that, in the second half of the 20th century, the social sciences have also started to study "subjective well-being" (SWB)[1]. The main contribution of the social sciences to life satisfaction research is to investigate "'empirically' measurable conditions, requirements, manifestations and consequences of happiness" (Bellebaum 2002: 15). In other words, researchers try to identify the „correlates of happiness" (Argyle 1999: 1) and to hypothesise about causal relationships.

The study of life satisfaction is part of a scientific branch called quality of life (QOL) research, which is an established field of

---

[1] As the remarks in chapter 2.1.3 and 2.1.4 will show, "subjective well-being", "happiness" and "life satisfaction" are actually distinct concepts, and precise definitions will be given. However, those terms will be used synonymously during the theoretical remarks in order to resort to a broader range of literature. Also, as some scholars argue, these concepts are closely related (Kahnemann 1999). Keck/Delhey (2004: 65) conclude that "as a rule of thumb, the results for happiness produce the same patterns as the findings for satisfaction". Likewise, summing up the results of various studies on SWB Haller/Hadler (2004) report happiness and life satisfaction to be very similar notions that correlate highly with each other.

empirical social research today. It has largely improved our understanding of the determinants of human well-being by developing theoretical models and empirical analyses on levels, changes and causes of well-being for different populations (Noll 2004). Within this framework, the question "why do people in some nations report to be more satisfied with their lives than in other nations" has challenged researchers and policy-makers alike for decades (see chapter 2.2). The standard approach to examine this phenomenon has so far been to correlate national mean SWB scores with material wealth, as measured by national product (Frey/Stutzer 2002). However, there are many shortcomings to this approach and it has increasingly been contested since Easterlin's (1974) famous objection „Does Economic Growth Improve the Human Lot?" Out of different kinds of criticism grew a new approach to studying the "well-being of nations"[2] (OECD 2001): the social capital approach. In the following book, many researchers' efforts to show a connection between social capital and SWB will be documented. This study will follow their footsteps by outlining the theoretical link between social capital and SWB, and by trying to explain differing national levels of life satisfaction with the amount of social capital in a society. In the end, the analysis based on data mainly from the World Values Survey (WVS) and the World Bank will find an answer the research question: *What are the effects of social capital on life satisfaction (at the cross-national level)?*

State of the Research

The development over the last 40 years of the two concepts investigated here, social capital and life satisfaction, has been remarkable. Before 1981, only 20 essays referred to social capital. Following the works of Coleman (1988) and Putnam (1993) this

---

[2] That is the name of the OECD's (2001) study examining the role of human and social capital for the QOL in many countries.

number grew to over 100 between 1991 and 1995. Finally, by 1999, more than 1,000 contributions dealt with social capital (Winter 2000). This has led some observers to even conclude that "social theory is being rewritten through the lens of social capital" (Fine 2000: 125). Likewise, when the study of life satisfaction started in the middle of the last century, it was overshadowed by research on negative states. In the 1960's, articles on the latter issue outnumbered those on SWB by 17:1 (Myers/Diener 1995). Since Wilson's seminal review (1967) on happiness, however, more than 300 studies on SWB had been conducted by the end of the 20th century (Diener et al. 1999). Today, at the beginning of the 21st century, there is "a large and rapidly growing body of research" that examines what makes people satisfied with their lives (Donovan et al. 2002: 2)[3].

The study of the QOL in general has gained not only theoretical, but also strong practical relevance over the last decades. Studies on the QOL provide societies – the general public as well as decision makers – with information needed for continuous self-reflection. It is consequently not surprising that QOL research today is well established within the information systems of many nation states and within international and supranational organisations like the OECD, the European Union, the World Health Organisation and the United Nations (Noll 2004, Power et al. 2002, Rapley 2003). Social capital has also received significant attention from policy-makers over the last decade. For example, the World Bank has investigated the effects of social capital in the context of economic progress and lately even developed its "Integrated Questionnaire on Social

[3] Particularly the journals "Social Indicators Research" and "Journal of Happiness Studies" provide a range of articles containing up-to-date research on QOL and SWB.

Capital" to measure it more precisely (World Bank 2004, see also OECD 2001).

Structure of the Book

In order to answer the research question, the following steps will be taken: First of all, the theoretical background (chapter 2) will outline the state of the research on the two concepts that will later be the dependent and independent variables - life satisfaction and social capital. To begin with, the concept of life satisfaction will be put in context and its choice as dependent variable will be discussed and justified. The introduction to the study of the QOL in general (2.1.1) will provide the reader with useful knowledge of the research field. It will be clarified how this study fits into the existing framework of QOL research by examining the different ways to measure QOL (2.1.2, 2.1.3), finally leading to generalised[4] life satisfaction (2.1.4). The second part of the theoretical background will summarise the state of the art concerning theories on SWB (2.2). To prove that the social capital approach was chosen with due thoughtfulness out of a range of prominent theories, those "other" approaches will be outlined and criticised first. Moreover, the theories will be discussed to examine if some need to be considered during the analysis later in the form of control variables. Central to the theoretical background is the chapter on the theoretical links from social capital to SWB (2.4), which follows after an introduction to social capital theory (2.3). Many previous studies in this area will be documented. Consequently, a firm theoretical and empirical basis for the subsequent hypotheses (3.) will be provided. Chapter 4 will then explain how the dependent, independent and control variables are

---

[4] The expression "generalised" means that the life satisfaction question is asked without reference to a certain life domain (see chapter 2.1.4). In the same manner, the "generalised trust" question enquires about trust towards people in general without reference to any particular group (see chapter 4.2).

operationalised, followed by the description of data and method (5.) with a special section dedicated to the challenges of conducting a cross-national analysis in this respect. Descriptive statistics (6.) and multivariate analyses (7.) will deliver results on the relationship between social capital and life satisfaction based on an investigation of all four waves of the World Values Survey. Those findings will be interpreted and discussed with regard to the hypotheses. Last but not least, conclusions (8.) will be drawn and implications for theory and policy that arise from the results shall be outlined[5].

---

[5] In this book there will be no physiological or biological account of processes that create a state of satisfaction or dissatisfaction. It shall only be stated that one of the points of broad agreement emerging from the literature on subjective well-being is that SWB is a composite of affective and cognitive processes (Gullone/Cummins 2002). In this book, respondents' answers to a survey question will be used as an empirical variable representing their state of life satisfaction (y). For further reading on the issue of how a state of satisfaction comes about in a physiological sense see Cummins et al. 2002, Frijda 1999, Nieboer/Lindenberg 2002, Schwarz/Strack 1999, Schumacher et al. 2003, Sirgy 2001.

2. Theoretical Background

2.1 Measuring Life Satisfaction

2.1.1 Quality of Life Research

"The great society is concerned not with how much, but with how good – not with the quantity of goods but with the quality of their lives."
U.S. President Lyndon B. Johnson, 1964 (as quoted in Rapley 2003: 4).

The research on the quality of life is assumed to remain in the core of sociological theory-building and empirical research at present and in the future (Genov 2004). Today, QOL research functions as an umbrella which unites people of similar research interests worldwide (Glatzer 2004). It was once developed as a more sophisticated and interdisciplinary concept to assess well-being in contrast to the simple measure of Gross Domestic Product (GDP)[6] per capita, especially facing the limits of further growth in industrialised countries. Since an initial study by the US space agency NASA in the 1960ies, research on the quality of life has received numerous

[6] GDP, Gross National Product (GNP) and Gross National Income (GNI) are measures of national income and output that are applied to estimate the value of goods and services produced in an economy. Since they all serve as indicators of the material wealth of a nation, they will be used interchangeably in this book. GDP is the total value of final goods and services produced within a country's borders in a year. GDP counts income according to where it is earned rather than who owns the factors of production. GNP is the total value of all final goods and services produced by a country's factors of production and sold on the market in a given time period. Last but not least, GNI comprises the total value of goods and services produced within a country, together with its income received from other countries (notably interest and dividends), less similar payments made to other countries (Black 2003).

contributions and its improvement has become a major goal of societal development (Glatzer 1992, Hagerty et al. 2002, Hirsch 1976, Mishan 1967, Noll 2004, Veenhoven 1996a)[7]. This new goal has today been adopted by governments, policy-makers, national and supranational institutions that are all running initiatives to measure and improve the QOL of their citizens (Berger-Schmitt/Noll 2000)[8]. Their efforts follow the "social indicators movement", once led by the OECD, the UN Social and Economic Council, as well as researchers such as Bertrand and Stone (Noll 2004, Rapley 2003).

The effects of the QOL illustrate why its improvement plays such a prominent role for governments, employers and human beings in general. For example, sharp declines in SWB preceded major constitutional changes in Belgium and the Soviet Union, or election losses for governments in many countries. One can therefore hypothesise that political change often was a direct consequence of decreasing levels of well-being (Hagerty 2002, Inglehart 1997, Inglehart/Klingemann 2000). Furthermore, happy people have been found to be more productive and economically more successful[9] (Graham et al. 2004). Satisfied employees work harder and more efficiently and have lower absence rates. SWB furthermore has positive effects on the length of life and mental health. However, it has to be noted that the direction of causation is not undisputed (Argyle 1996, see also Limitations, chapter 8.2).

---

7 For further reading on the history of QOL research see Land 1983, Noll 2000, 2004, Noll/Zapf 1994, Offer 1996, Rapley 2003, Sirgy et al. 2006).

8 For extensive overviews of surveys measuring the QOL see Braun 2002, Hudler/Richter 2002, Hudler-Seitzberger 2004, Noll 2004, Sirgy 2001, Veenhoven's "World Databank of Happiness" in Veenhoven 2004.

9 The causality can be assumed to run not only from economic success to happiness but also in this other way if we suppose that economic success is based on "certain psychological factors" (Glatzer 2004: 8, see also Kenny 1999).

Definitions of Quality of Life

QOL research has always been a multidisciplinary endeavour involving sociologists, statisticians, psychologists, economists, political scientists and policy-makers (Braun 2002). Furthermore, its multifaceted nature makes QOL a "shifting concept" (Glatzer 2004: 4), meaning it is used by different people in different respects: advertisers, for instance, claim to improve one's QOL if one buys a certain product, politicians promise before elections to raise the overall QOL in a country, etc. However, researchers attempt to clearly define it, measure it, and compare it cross-nationally (Glatzer 2004, Sirgy 2001). For example, Felce and Perry (1993) offer the following, widely accepted (Rapley 2003) definition for QOL:

> "Quality of life is defined as an overall general well-being which comprises objective descriptors and subjective evaluations of physical, material, social and emotional well-being together with the extent of personal development and purposeful activity all weighted by a personal set of values" (Felce/Perry 1993: 13).

In other words, the study of the quality of life today combines objective and subjective dimensions of social indicators to capture the life situation of individuals and groups (Noll 2004, Nussbaum/Sen 1993, Rapley 2003). Together with the separation of indicators, there are two schools of 'quality of life' or 'welfare' research: the Scandinavian, versus the American research tradition (see Noll 2000, 2004, Noll/Zapf 1994, Rapley 2003). The Scandinavian school of thought favours objective measures of well-being to assess one's level of living (see for example Erikson 1974, 1993, Drenowski 1974, Erikson/Uusitalo 1987, Uusitalo 1994), while the American approach concentrates on subjective measures as indicators for the QOL (Campbell et al. 1976). The former defines a high level of living as the "individual's command over resources

[…] such as income, wealth, knowledge, skills and health" (Erikson/Aberg 1987: 3). In contrast, the American school claims that the "quality of life must be in the eye of the beholder" (Campbell 1972: 442). QOL is defined as SWB and indicators are typically survey questions on life satisfaction, such as the one used in the following study. According to Noll,

> "the empirical correlates and explanatory factors of life satisfaction as an overall indicator of general subjective well-being are at the centre of [this] research field, which during recent years has attracted much interest and attention all around the world" (Noll 2004: 157).

Meanwhile, several scholars have attempted to overcome the divide between the two schools (Rapley 2003). For example, the Finnish sociologist Erik Allardt (1993) defines QOL in terms of „having, loving, being", i.e. the sum of material security, social relationships and personal self-expression. Likewise, Amatya Sen (1993) argues in favour of an approach that studies to which extent people are enabled to live in accordance with their "capabilities". Capabilities are defined as the freedom a person has to chose certain combinations of "functionings", i.e. the various "doings" and "beings" of a person (being well-nourished and disease-free, having self-respect and dignity, taking part in community life, etc.) that enable her or him to live a "thriving life" (Sen 1993). Likewise, Veenhoven (1996a) developed the index of "happy life-expectancy" combining the objective indicator life expectancy and subjectively reported happiness[10]. Consequently, the overall consensus in this science today is to base welfare measurement on both objective and

[10] Further approaches that combine objective and subjective measures are "Social Quality" (Walker/van der Maesen 2004), "Livability" (Veenhoven 1997), "Social Cohesion and Social Exclusion" (Noll 1999).

subjective indicators (Berger-Schmitt 2000, Christoph/Noll 2003, Delhey et al. 2002, Hudler/Richter 2002, Lane 1996, Noll 1999, 2004, Zapf 1984). Accordingly, Zapf (1984: 26) defines QOL as "good living conditions which go together with positive subjective well-being"[11].

This Study in the Framework of Quality of Life Research

Nonetheless, the distinction between objective and subjective indicators is still a central issue in QOL research. In fact, one's understanding of quality of life is determined by the indicator one uses (Offer 1996, Veenhoven 2002). Moreover, the choice of indicator can lead to remarkable differences in the resulting rankings of countries along their QOL[12] (Blanchflower/Oswald 2005). At this point, it makes sense to point out that the topic of this book is not "social capital and the *quality of life of nations*". For various reasons, people's subjective life satisfaction was chosen as dependent variable (see chapter 2.1.4). The following sub-chapters will therefore present causes and implications of choosing life satisfaction out of the range of indicators. At a glance, table 1 demonstrates how the dependent variable of this study (in bold) is embedded in the framework of QOL research[13]. As the table shows, the dependent variable used in the subsequent analysis, satisfaction with life as a whole, is a subjective indicator and as such part of the American QOL research tradition.

---

[11] The relationship between objective and subjective indicators of well-being will be investigated more precisely in chapter 2.2. For example, it will be examined to what extent a rising GNP (objective measure) increases peoples' life satisfaction (subjective measure).

[12] Australia, for instance, ranks very high on the UNDP Human Development Index every year, while it is considerably lower in international SWB-rankings (Blanchflower/Oswald 2005).

[13] A similar classification has been made by Cravens/Hills 1978: 53.

Table 1: Objective and Subjective Social Indicators

Frequently used objective social indicators (represent social data independently of individual evaluations): - Life expectancy - Crime rate - Unemployment rate - Gross Domestic Product - Poverty rate - School attendance - Working hours per week - Perinatal mortality rate - Suicide rate
Subjective social indicators (individual's appraisal and evaluation of social conditions): - Sense of community - Material possessions - Sense of safety - Happiness - **Satisfaction with "life as a whole"** - Relationships with family - Job satisfaction - Sex life - Perception of distributional justice - Class identification - Hobbies and club membership

Source: Items drawn from Cummins (1996); Hagerty et al. (2001) and Noll (2000); as published in Rapley 2003: 11. See the dependent variable (y) as used in the analysis here in bold.

A second fact becomes obvious in table 1: the explanatory variable social capital (here in the form of club membership[14]) can itself be an indicator for the QOL, again embedded within the American

[14] Precise definitions and operationalisations of social capital will be given in chapter 2.3.

school of thought. Nevertheless, since social capital is not a part of the concept of life satisfaction itself, the theoretical link from social capital to SWB remains to be explained (see chapter 2.4).

2.1.2 Objective Measures of Well-Being (Scandinavian Research Tradition)

Giving a more detailed overview on QOL research indicators, the next sub-chapters will explain what advantages and disadvantages each group of indicators has. Thereby will be justified why a subjective one was selected and what implications arise from this choice for the analysis.

The Nature of Objective Indicators

Objective indicators can in general be characterised by the fact that "the judgement of happiness is made according to external rules" from outside by the researcher (Frey/Stutzer 2002: 6). Objective measures can be divided into three groups: national product, extensions of national product and social indicators (ibid.)[15]. National product can be measured in GDP, GNI or GNP (see footnote 6). The attempt to develop a more refined measure led to the creation of extensions of national product. These measures take into account the disadvantages of economic success such as the costs of pollution, crime, divorce, etc. (see for example "Measure of Economic Welfare" by Nordhaus/Tobin 1972, "Index of Sustainable Economic Welfare" by Daly/Cobb 1989 and "Economic Aspects of Welfare" by Zolotas (1981), as quoted in Frey/Stutzer 2002). Social indicators stand for a related concept, assuming that people who

[15] Furthermore, objective indicators for the well-being of a particular individual can be measuring brain waves physiologically by using a hedonometer (Frey/Stutzer 2002), or determining the levels of dopamine and serotonine in the body (Ebstein et al. 1996).

have access to certain goods like nutrition, housing, health or education are satisfied with their lives. Social indicators can be defined as "statistics that usefully reflect important social conditions and that facilitate the process of assessing those conditions and their evolution" (United Nations 1994 as quoted in Noll 2004: 4). Today there is an extensive research on social indicators, e.g. the UK's annual "Social Trends" (since 1970), France's "*Données Sociales*" (since 1973) or Germany's "*Datenreport*" (since 1983) (Frey/Stutzer 2002, Rapley 2003).

In general, objective measures like GNP and GDP are standard measures of economic development today and are frequently used to assess societal levels of well-being in many (especially economic) publications (Nussbaum/Sen 1993). The United Nations, for example, use GNP as a measure in 1948 in order to compare the development of different countries[16], and the World Bank still relies mainly on national product in order to assess countries in development rankings.

Advantages of Objective Measures

Adjusted to power-purchasing-parity (PPP), GDP per capita scores of nations have the advantage of being easily put side by side. Without a doubt, the precise comparability of their scores across countries and their nature to be considered as 'hard facts' have earned objective indicators their central place in QOL assessments. Compared to subjective indicators, there are no memory biases or similar problems that such retrospective self-reports suffer from (Frey/Stutzer 2002, Noll 2004, Rapley 2003).

[16] Meanwhile, the UN work with a different indicator for the QOL of nations, the "Human Development Index" (UNDP 1990).

Disadvantages of Objective Measures
On the other hand, the prominent use of national product in policy-making is disputed:

> "Most social scientists and economists would agree that GNP is a crude and incomplete measure of the quality of life; and yet those measures continue to be widely used when public policy is made" (Nussbaum/Sen 1993: 2).

GNP is problematic because it does not give any information about how the wealth in a country is distributed among its inhabitants, nor if the money is invested to improve the QOL of the people (ibid). In general, objective indicators have one central weakness: the normative judgment from outside, i.e. of the researcher who conducts the study. It is the scientist who defines a desirable state ("the good life", "the good society"), and then assesses to what extent the cases are in compliance with that ideal. Hence, "in order to measure the quality of life, one must have a theory of what makes up a good life" (Cobb 2000: 6).

More precisely, objective measures of well-being rely on the assumption that there is societal consensus about three issues: first, consensus about the dimensions of a society that need to be studied in order to assess its quality of life; second, what would be bad and what would be good conditions to live in; and third, the goal that society should develop towards (Noll 2004). Only if these three criteria are met and agreed upon, the concept of objective measures can be applied successfully. Whereas the consensus may be easily reached for uncontroversial indicators such as access to fresh drinking water or low child mortality, it is not so easily accomplished for other ones such as divorce rates, income, equality and many more. In other words, no advocate of subjective measures of well-being would doubt that objective indicators like the crime rate or life expectancy can appropriately represent the well-being of citizens in any given country. But the problem of objective indicators becomes obvious when the normative idea of "the good society" is culturally (or even sub-culturally) relative, or if it harbours political and ideological opinion (Rapley 2003).

It is, for example, controversial whether high divorce rates are primarily an indicator of many disturbed relationships in a society, and consequently signify a low QOL. Or are they rather a positive fact, indicating that people are allowed to lead self-determined lives and have the freedom to end a relationship when they want to, thus pointing towards a high QOL? Subjective indicators, on the contrary, allow those affected by divorce to judge for themselves whether it makes them happier or not[17]. Another example is: how much permanent income does a person need in order to be satisfied? The answers vary enormously according to someone's aspirations which are not taken into account by objective indicators (Diener/Suh 1999, Inglehart 1990, Kenny 2005). Last but not least, in addition to the external living conditions, well-being depends on whether the individuals themselves actually give their life some quality (Lane 1996).

To conclude, objective measures "are strongly normative judgements in the sense that happiness is assessed according to fixed rules, although our attitude toward particular pleasures and pains is not a priori given" (Frey/Stutzer 2002: 6). People, on the other hand, may evaluate certain objective goods as more or less beneficial to their personal life satisfaction. The philosopher Robert Nozick (1989) described the problem as follows: it is difficult to assume that

[17] As far as divorce and SWB are concerned it has been revealed that differences in life satisfaction between complete and single parent families are in fact extremely small (Lont/Dronkers 2004).

certain things will make people happy as diverse as Marilyn Monroe, Albert Einstein, Ludwig Wittgenstein and Louis Armstrong. Subjective indicators therefore leave it open to the interviewed person to define and evaluate what makes him or herself happy. So instead of dictating what "the good life" consists of (a certain income level, a high or a low divorce rate, etc.), the researcher can just ask people to evaluate for themselves how satisfied they are with their life situations. In this sense, "it can be assumed that [people themselves] are the best judges of when they are happy and when they are unhappy" (Frey/Stutzer 2002: 4).

2.1.3 Subjective Measures of Well-Being (American Research Tradition)

The Nature of Subjective Measures

Demands to assess people's well-being by simply asking them about it go back to Aristotle (384 BC – 322 BC), who argued that:

> "We must therefore *survey* what we have already said [about what "the good life" objectively consists of], bringing it to the test of the facts of life, and if it harmonises with the facts we must accept it, but if it clashes with them we must suppose it to be mere theory" (Nicomachean Ethics, Book 10, 1179: 23 as quoted in Helliwell 2003: 333).

The pioneer studies on subjective life satisfaction of Andrews and Whitey (1976) and Campbell et al. (1976) have given rise to an immense literature (Rapley 2003). Moreover, some researchers argue for SWB rankings to play an even more prominent role in policy planning today (see for example Diener 2000, Offer 2000,

Veenhoven 2002, Vemuri/Constanza 2006). The term "subjective well-being" [18] is defined as:

> "people's evaluations of their lives, and includes variables such as life satisfaction, the frequent experience of pleasant emotions, the infrequent experience of unpleasant emotions, satisfaction with domains such as marriage and work, and feelings of fulfilment and meaning" (Diener/Oishi 2004: 1).

All in all, subjective measures "emphasise the individual perception and evaluation of social conditions" (Noll 2000: 1). To gain a better understanding about how we can measure SWB, Blanchflower/ Oswald (2000) suggested to formalise the concept as shown in figure 1.

SWB is typically assessed with surveys that can contain multiple-item or single-item questions. Respondents are asked to evaluate their general life satisfaction, happiness, satisfaction with a certain domain (e.g. job, family, leisure), etc. A widely used generalised single-item question is for instance: "All things considered, how satisfied are you with your life as a whole these days?" Respondents can rate themselves on a scale from 1 (completely dissatisfied) to 10 (completely satisfied). Another option is to ask: "Taken all together, how happy would you say you are? Very happy, quite happy, not very happy or not at all happy?" Whereas single-item questions capture a general trend, multiple-item questions can investigate different dimensions of well-being (Diener et al. 1999, Frey/Stutzer 2002).

---

[18] In economics, the concept of SWB also called "utility", as established by Jeremy Bentham (1748-1832) and John Stuart Mill (1806-1876) (Frey/Stutzer 2002, Nussbaum/Sen 1993).

$$r = h(u(y, z, t)) + e$$

r =	self-reported score of well-being as expressed by the respondent
h =	function relating actual well-being to reported well-being
u =	the respondent's actual well-being
y =	real income
z =	a set of demographic and personal characteristics
t =	time period
e =	error term, representing factors that influence the relationship between actual and reported well-being

Figure 1: Equation of SWB. Source: Blanchflower/Oswald (2000): 3.

Among the multiple-item questions, probably the most prominent one is the "Satisfaction with Life Scale" (Diener et al. 1985, Pavot/Diener 1993). Respondents are asked to indicate their level of agreement on a scale from 1 to 7 with five items such as "I am satisfied with my life" or "If I could live my life over, I would change almost nothing". Moreover, surveys may enquire about feelings of depression or excitement over a certain period of time. Several scales to measure SWB using multiple items have been developed in the past such as the "Affect Balance Scale" (ABS) (Bradburn 1969), the "Positive and Negative Affect Schedule" (PANAS) (Watson et al. 1988), and the "Pleasant Affect/ Unpleasant Affect Scale" (Diener/Emmons 1985). All in all, in an analysis of 32 studies Cummins (1996) identified 173 different life satisfaction questions. The choice of measurement instrument finally depends on the nature and purpose of the research project. Veenhoven (1996a), however, identified the generalised happiness question to be the most commonly used item.

Advantages of Subjective Indicators

Referring to what has been said about the disadvantages of objective indicators of well-being, subjective indicators do not impose a normative judgment from outside, but allow the respondent to evaluate the quality of life him- or herself. In other words, respondents are allowed to judge to which extent certain objective conditions affect their own well-being. Subjective measures take into account each individual's aspiration level and needs in assessing their level of life satisfaction. For instance, some people appreciate a lot of consumer choice to be satisfied, whereas others might be overwhelmed by the same amount of choice (see Inglehart/Welzel 2005, Offer 2006). What seems to be more important to somebody's well-being than the outside conditions is how that person perceives and evaluates these conditions. People in bad conditions can be satisfied, and privileged persons may be very dissatisfied (Christoph/Noll 2003, Zapf 1984). Furthermore, people's social comparisons with reference groups influence their degree of life satisfaction. Social comparisons are not taken into account in objective assessments but can be reflected in subjective statements (Clark/Oswald 1996, Diener/Suh 1999, Frey/Stutzer 2002, Neumark/Postlewaite 1998).

Scholars have concluded that SWB is a sufficiently reliable and valid statistical measure, since individuals' responses to survey questions on SWB have proven to be moderately stable and appropriately sensitive to changing life circumstances. In other words, "subjective indicators measure what they ought to measure and they react sensitive to societal development" (Habich/Zapf 1994: 30). Furthermore, possible biases[19], e.g. social desirability, unfamiliarity with the concept of life satisfaction or happiness, etc.

[19] Potential cultural biases will be discussed in section 2.2 (Cultural Approach) and chapter 5 (Challenges of a Cross-National Analysis) of this book.

were not found to have a significant influence on SWB scores in various investigations (Habich/Zapf 1994, Headey/Wearing 1992, Helliwell/Putnam 2004, Frey/Stutzer 2002, Noll 2004).

Last but not least, subjective indicators of well-being have proven to be consistent[20] with a range of other measures of well-being: There is empirical consistency between a person's subjectively expressed well-being and third party observations (i.e. judgements about the person's well-being by friends, relatives or spouse). High correlations were also found with the amount of positive versus negative memories the respondent recalls, as well as with physiological and behavioural measures such as brain waves, hormones (endorphins), frequency of smiling or walking upright. Furthermore, objective indicators like low absenteeism from work and a low suicide rate in a country also correlate positively with SWB (Argyle 1996, Balatsky/Diener 1993, Diener 2000, Diener/Suh 1999, Donovan et al. 2002, Frey/Stutzer 2002, Helliwell 2001, 2006, Helliwell/Putnam 2004, Sandvik et al. 1993, Wilson 1967).

In summary, the findings of numerous studies have identified life satisfaction to have very plausible relationships with a host of other variables. "It is this body of consistent findings that is ultimately the strongest source of validity for life satisfaction as a measure, and that drives growing academic and policy interest in the concept" (Donovan et al. 2002: 8).

Disadvantages of Subjective Indicators

All subjective survey data is subject to a range of disadvantages. A respondent's answer can be influenced by: ordering effects (here especially what item precedes the life satisfaction question), wording

[20] In this case, consistency means the extent to which respondents' statements about their subjective life satisfaction correspond to other measures of well-being.

effects (i.e. the words used in the question), scale effects (i.e. the type of scale used), social desirability and cognitive dissonance (i.e. expressed attitudes and actual behaviour are not consistent). All those factors are known to distort the "true" score of a person (see the error term ε in the equation by Blanchflower/Oswald 2000 in figure 1; see also Bertrand/ Mullainathan 2001, Hudler/Richter 2002, Sudman et al. 1996). The data collection procedure is another critical point. The behaviour of the interviewer might unwillingly influence respondents' answers (Michalos 1992). Sudman et al. (1967) found that people report to be happier in face-to-face interviews compared to paper questionnaires (see also Saris et al. 1998, Scherpenzeel/Saris 1997). However, this argument has been doubted in a replication by Diener/Suh (1999). Finally, while some argue for the translations to influence the comparability of survey results (Hambleton/Patsula 1998), findings from cross-national surveys involving multilingual countries disprove this point (see chapter 2.2, Linguistic Approaches).

Even one of the advantages of subjective measures of well-being, i.e. that it takes into account the individual's own evaluation of his or her living conditions, can be considered a disadvantage if viewed from a different angle. As the Scandinavian welfare researcher Erikson (1993) points out, the problem with an approach based on people's own assessment of their degree of satisfaction is that it is partly determined by their level of aspiration. Therefore people's SWB only indicates how well they are adapted to their present conditions. This can especially be a problem when interpreting the SWB of people in underdeveloped countries, since people's aspirations may be limited by a lifetime of deprivation and lack of education, and they are adapted to very low standards (Camfield 2004, Jayawardena 1993)[21]. The same may be true for extremely

[21] Lane (1991) described this problem as accepting the 'wantlessness' of the poor.

rich people whose aspirations have adapted to extraordinarily high standards. This phenomenon is called "adaptation" in the literature (e.g. Offer 1996) and can be illustrated in the following way:

> "Adaptation has two aspects: goods may loose their appeal, while bads lose their bite, leading, ultimately, to the 'happy slave' syndrome, or to Ivan Denisovich, Solzhenitsyn's labour camp inmate who looks back with satisfaction on a good day, in which nothing worse than the usual deprivations took place" (Offer 1996: 13).

On the other hand, the feelings of satisfaction, respectively dissatisfaction, which even those deviant rich or poor people express in surveys, may be heartfelt because if people "define situations as real, they are real in their consequences" (Thomas/Thomas 1928: 572). That is to say, their subjectively expressed level of life satisfaction can be considered an appropriate image of their perceived QOL in this case. In a similar fashion, doubts are raised whether survey data can be compared across individuals and nations (concerning cross-national comparability see a detailed discussion in chapter 5). In other words, do we all mean the same by "satisfied"? However, in large samples those differences in interpretation are less of a problem since they occur fairly randomly (Donovan et al. 2002).

Serious methodological concerns finally deal with the question whether feelings can accurately be quantified into surveys' metric scales by respondents. SWB measures presuppose that people are conscious of and able to articulate nuances of feelings (Cobb 2000). Furthermore there are several memory biases and situational influences that the respondent's answer can be subject to. The response to the generalised life satisfaction question for example is made under the influence of the life domains that the individual has most recently been thinking about (Cutler et al. 1996, Diener/Fujita

1995, Kahnemann 1999)[22]. In a similar way, Schwarz/Strack (1999: 61) claim that survey responses on SWB questions were made on the basis of spontaneous judgements "on the spot", assigning a large influence on the outcome score to whether a happy rather than sad event comes to mind of the respondent. Other researchers, on the contrary, claim that respondents were not strongly influenced by their current moods when making life satisfaction judgements, nor were people reluctant to use the extremes of the scale (Diener/Suh 1999, Pavot/Diener 1993).

2.1.4 Generalised Life Satisfaction

Life satisfaction in particular can be defined "as the degree to which an individual evaluates the overall quality of his or her life as favourable" (Vittersø et al. 2002: 81). According to Veenhoven (1991) life satisfaction "is conceived as the degree to which an individual judges the overall quality of his life-as-a-whole favourably. In other words: how well he likes the life he leads."

It has been argued that an assessment of life satisfaction needs to have at least 3-5 items because emotional states could not be expressed by a single answer (Diener et al. 1985, Pavot/Diener 1993). Furthermore, single-item questions may have a risk of "over-simplifying" things (Diener/Suh 1997). However, the generalised life satisfaction question correlates highly with other, more elaborate surveys (convergent validity) such as the General Health Questionnaire (GHQ) (Rapley 2003). That is to say the generalised life satisfaction question and multiple-item questionnaires, as well as

[22] Kahnemann (1999) therefore suggests an alterntive measure: a person's "objective happiness", defined as the average of utility over a period of time of an individual; unfortunately, large cross-national surveys such as the World Values Survey do not include such time series data for certain individuals.

more sophisticated mental health scales, are empirically consistent. Consequently, multiple-domain life satisfaction measures have even been termed "essentially redundant" (ibid.: 15), since comparative meta-analysis of eleven large-scale studies resulted in "sufficiently close relationships" between scores on single-item measures and the aggregate scores of multiple-domain measures.

In conclusion, Andrews and Withey's (1976) generalised question: "How do you feel about your life as a whole?" is widely used as a QOL index and one of the few empirical benchmarks of QOL research (Cummins 1996, Rapley 2003)[23]. Moreover, psychological research has shown that a person's state of happiness can be adequately captured by such a single summary measure (Kahnemann 1999). The overall evaluation of life satisfaction demonstrates significant intrapersonal stability and interpersonal comparability (Frey/Stutzer 2002). In summary, "it is empirically possible for most individuals to evaluate their life as a whole" (van Praag/Frijters 1999: 427).

Life Satisfaction vs. Happiness

While many analysts use the terms life satisfaction and happiness synonymously, the distinction shall be pointed out here at least once, in order to inform the reader of its existence and to explain why life satisfaction was chosen as dependent variable instead of happiness. Campbell et al. (1976) argue that life satisfaction is a more reliable concept than happiness because it is a cognitive judgement, whereas happiness refers to a feeling of affect. Lane (2000) supports this statement by arguing that happiness is a mood while satisfaction with life is a more cognitive evaluation. That is to say, research has

[23] Another more practical reason for using the generalised life satisfaction question is that "there is a large body of such evidence already to hand, and the question is so simple to ask" (Helliwell 2003: 332).

identified responses to the happiness question to be more of an emotional nature that correlates with recent experiences of fun and a good family life (Andrews/Whitey 1976, Sirgy 2001). On the other hand, respondents take into account their overall life situation, like for example their financial situation, when answering life satisfaction questions (Campbell et al. 1976, Gundelach/Kreiner 2004, Inglehart/Rabier 1986, Michalos 1985, Sirgy 2001). It can be concluded in line with a similar analysis by Helliwell/Putnam (2004: 1438):

> "in short, the 'life satisfaction' measure seems marginally better than the 'happiness' measure for our purposes of estimating the effects of relatively stable features of social context (and especially social capital), but broadly speaking, our central results do not depend on the choice of indicators of subjective well-being" (ibid.).

Since this investigation focuses rather on mindful assessments of respondents' life situation than on "gut reactions" (Sirgy 2001: 31), life satisfaction seems to be the better variable for the purpose of this study. In addition, the correlation with social capital can be expected to provide more promising results using a dependent variable based on cognitive evaluation of one's overall situation and surroundings.

With regard to the points that have been made so far concerning QOL indicators, the choice of the dependent variable should now seem justified and its chances and limitations have been pointed out. The implication for this study is to keep such criticism in mind when drawing conclusions from the empirical results. All in all, although subjective indicators have potential disadvantages, this book will comply with the "professional consensus", according to which the responses to the life satisfaction question, "though not without their problems, are meaningful and reasonably comparable among groups of individuals" (Easterlin 2004: 347, see also Diener 1984, Frey/Stutzer 2002, Veenhoven 1993).

In conclusion, the research field as it has been discussed in the preceding chapters can be visualised as in figure 2. While the focus has so far been on locating and investigating the QOL-indicator "generalised life satisfaction" within the framework of QOL research, the subsequent chapter will focus on how to explain differences in life satisfaction levels.

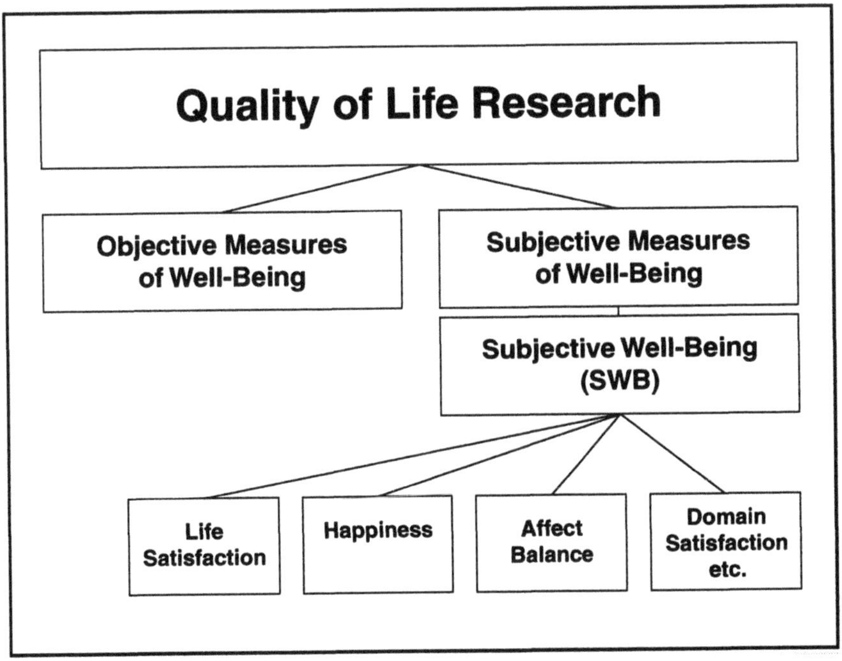

Figure 2: The basic framework of QOL research as discussed in this book.

2.2 Theoretical Approaches to Explain Differences in Subjective Well-Being (SWB)

The international differences in SWB are quite remarkable. In cross-national studies, national mean life satisfaction scores usually range between ca. 3 and 8 on a scale from 1 to 10 (see for example Delhey 2004, Diener et al. 1995a, 1995b, Donovan et al. 2002, Inglehart 1990, Inglehart/Klingemann 2000, Weller 1996; see also chapter 6 and appendix of this book). In addition, Inglehart (1990) observed that variations of SWB scores were minimal within nations but high across nations (see also Donovan et al. 2002, Weller 1996)[24].

This chapter will serve to give the reader an overview of the state of research on explaining differences in life satisfaction. Since the subsequent study is at the cross-national level, the approaches for the individual level will be presented in brief, followed by a more detailed section for the cross-national level. For each respective level of analysis, the most prominent theoretical approaches will be presented more or less in order of growing plausibility. Important factors discussed here need to be considered in the analysis later as control variables. In order to be able to resort to a wider range of literature and because the concepts are indeed closely related (see footnote 1), all facets of SWB will continuously be included in the theoretical remarks, while the empirical part will focus on life satisfaction.

---

[24] Easterlin (2000: 4), on the other hand, argued for macroeconomic and political influences from the 'public sphere' not to have an influence on individuals' well-being. He claimed that people take their societal surroundings such as social equality, political stability and GDP as a 'given' that they cannot influence anyways, contrary to their personal domains such as family life, leisure or work. However, as the international differences in SWB and their correlations with macroeconomic factors show in this chapter, societal factors do exercise a certain influence on the SWB of people.

Which theories have been brought forward in the literature to explain differences in SWB scores? At the individual level, biologists argue that genes have a determining effect on one's level of life satisfaction, and therefore view happiness as a trait that one can either have or not. Each individual has a "set-point" of SWB, determined by genetics and personality. The satisfaction level always returns to this point, even after changing life circumstances such as marriage, divorce or a pay rise (Brickman et al. 1978, Costa et al. 1987, Cummins et al. 2002, Grinde 2002a, 2002b, Lucas 2007, Lykken/Tellegen 1996, Stones et al. 1995, Tellegen et al. 1988, Tversky/Griffin 1991). These are certainly plausible points. However, as Klingemann/Inglehart (2000) and Veenhoven (1994) demonstrated, the limitations of the explanatory power of genes become obvious when genes fail to explain the systematic, international differences in SWB. According to those authors, cross-national differences can only be assigned to societal factors.

Psychologists stress the importance of cognitive strategies such as a small goal-achievement gap, attribution of good events to the self and bad events to others (psychic hygiene), goal attainment and personality traits like extroversion for determining somebody's level of life satisfaction (Argyle 1987, Diener/Lucas 1999, Emmons/ Diener 1985, Kahnemann 1999, Ratzlaff et al. 2000, Seligmann 2002). The psychological experience of "flow", i.e. satisfaction arising from temporary life events, was also reported to enhance life satisfaction[25] (Csikszentmihalyi 1997, Headey/Wearing 1992,

[25] The psychological literature distinguishes satisfaction as derived from temporary events ("flow"), versus derived from stable characteristics like personality traits (e.g. extraversion, low neuroticism) or the social background (economic status, age, etc.). The latter are called the "stocks" of happiness (Kahnemann 1999). Since correlations of SWB with stable characteristics such as membership and interpersonal trust are central to this analysis, it can be categorised as investigating the "stocks" dimension.

Kahnemann 1999). These influences on SWB may be important, however, it takes surveys with a range of specific variables to measure those dimensions. The World Values Survey (WVS) and other broad cross-national surveys do not contain such data.

Finally, sociologists, economists and social psychologists mainly focus on demographic attributes of satisfied people. The most important correlates at the individual level are work (for instance an interesting job and nice colleagues), family life, health, age, occupational status, social status, leisure, marital status, income (especially relative, not absolute income), religiosity, education, intelligence, and frequency of physical activities (Argyle 1996, 1999, Diener et al. 1999, Easterlin 2004, Fisch 2002, Frey/Stutzer 2002, Hettlage 2002, Layard 2005, Myers 2000)[26]. Social relationships and support, however, were frequently found to have the biggest effect on SWB in most studies (Donovan et al. 2002). Various researchers claim that some of those correlates of SWB correspond to various human needs and have even tried to rank such desires (see Maslow's "hierarchy of needs" (1981); see also Fisch 2002, Stewart 1996). In an initial study, Wilson (1967: 294) described the ideal type of a happy person as a "young, healthy, well-educated, well-paid, extroverted, optimistic, worry-free, religious, married person with high self-esteem, job morale, modest aspirations, of either sex and of a wide range of intelligence", based on the "correlates of avowed happiness".

At the cross-national level, too, a range of theories can be identified in the literature. They shall be discussed in the following section as a basis for the subsequent empirical analysis.

---

[26] Please note that in this study, men and women are not differentiated. For gender differences on the sources of well-being see for example Nolen-Hoeksema/Rusting (1999).

Linguistic Approach

Starting with an obvious assumption, one could claim that the differing levels of life satisfaction across countries are due to the fact that the meaning of "satisfied with your life" varies from one language to another. Indeed, "satisfied" may have different connotations than "*zufrieden*" or "*satisfait*". However, cross-national studies involving multilingual countries such as Belgium or Switzerland showed that this is not the case in empirical research. The French-speaking Belgians, for example, gave answers closer to the Dutch-speaking Belgians than to the French. The same was true for the Swiss, whose answers were countrywide fairly homogenous across language barriers, and were consistently higher than those of their French or German neighbours. Hence, several authors concluded that nationality is the determining factor in predicting the SWB score of a respondent, prior to his or her language affiliation, as indicated by the results mentioned here (Inglehart 1990, Inglehart/Rabier 1986, Layard 2005, Ouweneel/ Veenhoven 1991, Veenhoven 1993).

Cultural Approach

A second approach to explaining international differences in SWB is the cultural one. According to this view, the social norm to present oneself as happy varies across countries. In other words, the "societal structures of norms and values on which depends, to what extent a state of positive, subjective well-being is demanded normatively" differ between nations (Noll 1997: 462; see also Diener/Suh 1999, Inglehart 1990, Noll 2000, Suh et al. 1998, Triandis 2000, Vittersø et al. 2002, Zapf 1984). Some authors even concluded that most of the cross-national differences in SWB were due to cultural factors. Ostroot/Snyder (1985), for instance, claimed that the differences in the national mean scores between the USA and France were largely due to such a cultural influence. Veenhoven

(1987), on the other hand, doubted those findings and drew attention to aspects of societal quality.

In summary, there seems to be a cultural component. However, its effects on life satisfaction scores are equally hard to prove, since no reliable measure for these cultural norms has been developed yet.

Values Approach

Another school of thought draws attention to societal values and investigates to which extent people perceive these values to be accomplished in their environment. In other words, do people's aspirations for their lives (ideal self) correspond to their real lives (actual self) (Sirgy 2001)? Quality of life would thus be the extent to which hopes and ambitions are matched by experience (Calman 1987, Michalos 1986, Schwartz/Melech 2000). Unfortunately, this complex issue needs measurement of both subjective ambitions and experiences, and research on it is still in its infancy (see for example the "goal attainment theory" in Diener/Suh 1999, Oishi/Diener 2001).

Political Approach

It can be assumed that human rights, political freedom and democratic institutions contribute to people's SWB. If people are protected by law, have the chance to elect (and not re-elect) their government, and can live without the fear of being arrested without acceptable reasons, they should feel more secure and more satisfied. Furthermore, they should enjoy more rights to self-fulfilment, for example through participation and the right to go on strike (Cummins 2001, Diener et al. 1995b, Frey/Al-Roumi 1999, Lane 2000). Accordingly, the lowest national mean SWB score ever measured in history was 1962 in the Dominican Republic, during a time of political riot and civil unrest (Frey/Stutzer 2002).

Frey/Stutzer (2002) reported that cantons in Switzerland which allow more direct political participation through referenda have significantly higher mean levels of SWB. Moreover, the quality of government was found to be closely linked to national mean SWB (Helliwell/Huang 2006). Likewise, a human rights index correlates with SWB across nations at r = 0.48 (Diener et al. 1995b). Political and economic freedom were also associated with SWB across nations (Haller/Hadler 2004, Inglehart/Welzel 2005, Veenhoven 2000). The "Freedom House Index", which captures the degree of civil liberties and political rights in countries, in fact highly correlates with national SWB scores measured by the World Values Survey in a bivariate analysis (Inglehart/Klingemann 2000), as pictured in figure 3. As illustrated, the degree of democratisation is positively associated with the nations' SWB scores with a remarkable r = 0.78. However, it needs to be pointed out that some examples give reason to doubt the relationship between democracy and happiness. China, for instance, can compensate for the lack of democracy through its economic growth over the last decades. Similarly, since the collapse of the Soviet Union, the SWB score of Russia has declined sharply despite a democratisation process, probably due to economic decline, ideological disillusionment and rising crime rates (Inglehart/Klingemann 2000).

After all, the degree of democratisation covaries with other factors that can increase SWB, such as national product (Diener/Suh 1999). Its independent effect still has not been proven in a multivariate analysis. In conclusion, due to the expected collinearity with material wealth it does not seem appropriate to include the degree of democratisation as a control variable later if variables of national product are present in the regression analysis[27].

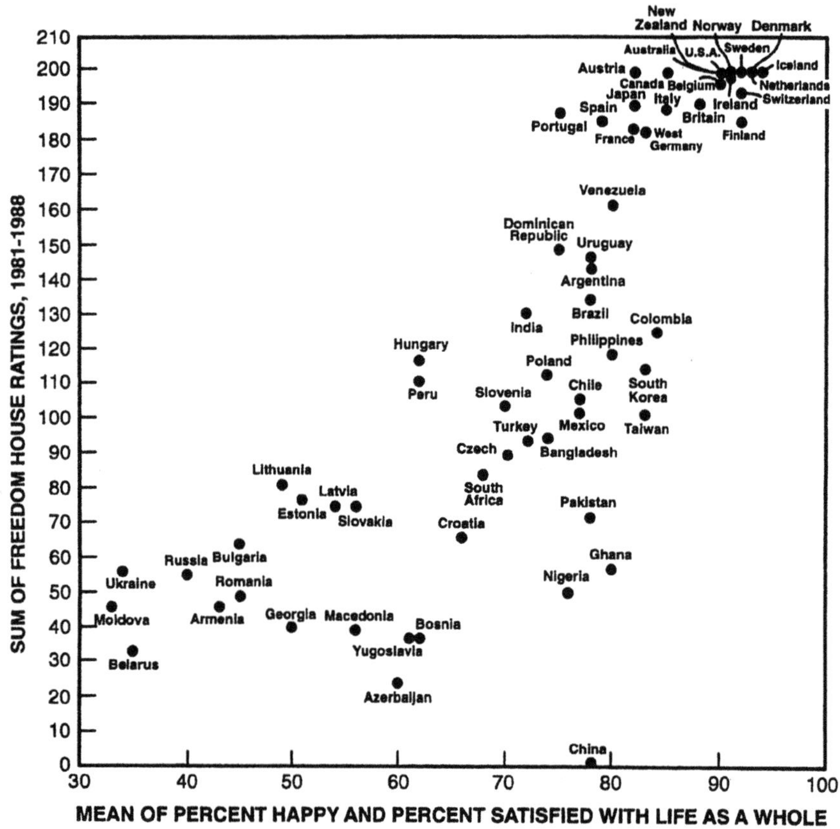

Figure 3: SWB and democratic institutions; r = 0.78, p = 0.00, N = 62. Source: Inglehart/Klingemann 2000: 178.

[27] A bivariate correlation indeed shows that the GDP per capita and the Freedom House Index are closely associated (r > 0.6), see appendix. Collinearity between two independent variables would lead to distorted coefficients (Brosius 2006).

Economic Approach

GNP and SWB

As mentioned in the beginning of this book, GNP is the standard measure when trying to explain cross-national differences in mean levels of SWB and will therefore be discussed in detail here (Diener et al. 1993, 1995b, 1999, Diener/Oishi 2000, Di Tella et al. 2001, Gallup 1976, Hagerty/Veenhoven 2003, Headey/Wearing 1992, Inglehart 1990, Inglehart/Klingemann 2000, Inglehart/ Welzel 2005, Kenny 2005, Veenhoven 1997; GNP, GDP and GNI are used synonymously, see footnote 6). In fact, the bivariate correlation as reported by Inglehart/Klingemann (2000) using data from the World Bank and the World Values Survey, is significant and lies at an acceptable r = 0.70, see figure 4.

Also highlighting a connection between national product and SWB in a cross-national study, Cantril (1967) reported a correlation between his index of economic development and SWB in 14 countries with r = 0.67. The mean income in 28 nations and the average SWB in them correlated at r = 0.62 in a study by Ouweneel/Veenhoven (1991), and Diener et al. (1995a) reported it to be r = 0.59 for their sample of 55 nations. Schyns (1998) finally discovered a correlation of r = 0.64 between GDP and happiness scores in his analysis of 36 nations.

Nonetheless, there are many points of criticism. They need to be discussed in the following paragraphs because the shortcomings of the economic approach partly justify the choice of the social capital approach for the subsequent empirical analysis. First, there are outliers with a higher SWB score than their GNP would predict, for example Colombia, Ghana or the Philippines as shown in figure 4. This phenomenon has been called "paradox of poverty", "satisfaction paradox", "disability paradox" (Rapley 2003: 31) or "adaptation" (Noll 1997: 467; Zapf 1984). In fact, these nations'

SWB scores are ranked above some European countries' although the GNPs of the latter are more than 10 times higher (see for instance Philippines vs. West Germany).

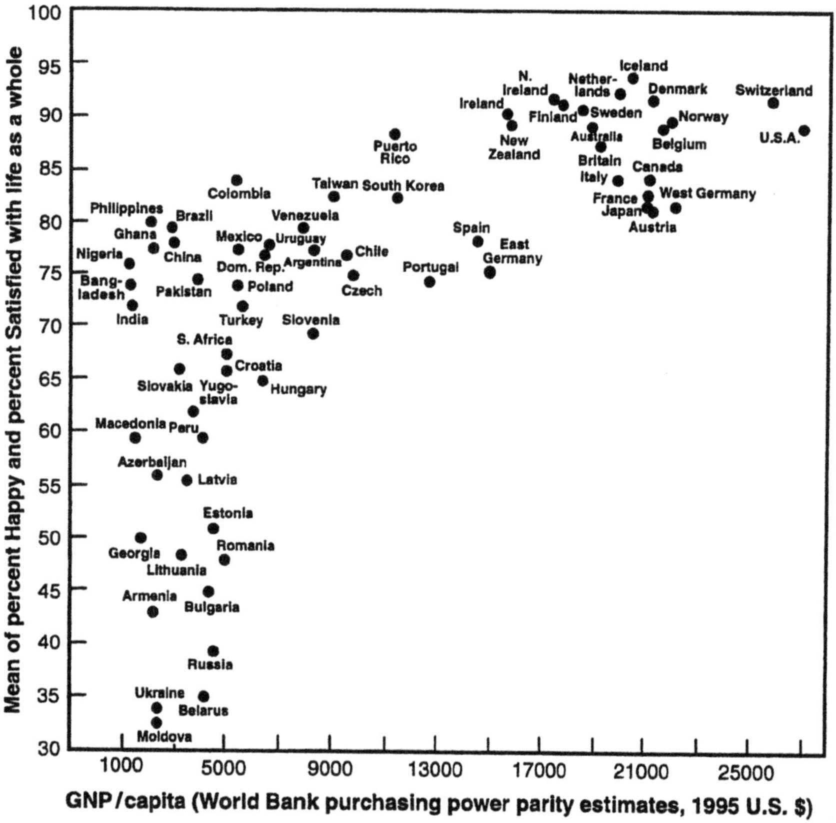

Figure 4: SWB by level of economic development; r = 0.70, p = 0.00, N = 65. Source: Inglehart/Klingemann 2000: 168.

Second, there are outliers whose SWB scores are lower than their GNP would predict. This phenomenon is called the "dissatisfaction dilemma“ (Rapley 2003: 31) or “dissonance” (Noll 1997: 467, Zapf 1984). Noll (1997) identified Italy and France[28] as belonging to this group within Europe. A classification scheme developed by Zapf (1984) demonstrates how the relationship between GNP and SWB can be illustrated. The terms adaptation and dissonance as discussed here can be found in table 2.

Table 2: Dimensions of Objective and Subjective Well-Being

Objective Living Conditions	Subjective Well-being	
	Good	Bad
Good	WELL-BEING	DISSONANCE
Bad	ADAPTATION	DEPRIVATION

Source: Zapf 1984: 25.

A major point of criticism towards the economic approach is that the correlation between GNP and SWB completely diminishes for countries above $ 13,000 per capita. Consequently, no relationship between those two variables can be found for the richest countries (Inglehart/Klingemann 2000). Already in a 1974 study, Easterlin could not find a correlation between GDP and SWB in a sample including the 15 richest nations. This phenomenon is since then also called the “income-happiness paradox” (Diener/Oishi 2000, Easterlin 1974, Frey/Stutzer 2002) and can be illustrated by looking

[28] Without giving away the results of the empirical analysis involving social capital, it can already be said that these two countries also rank relatively low on interpersonal trust. This fact points to the assumption that social capital is a better predictor for SWB than is GDP.

at a time series that compares GDP with life satisfaction in the United Kingdom, for instance. Although GDP has grown enormously between 1975 and 1996, the national mean life satisfaction remains nearly unchanged (figure 5). Blanchflower/ Oswald (2000) even claim for Americans' reported happiness to have fallen since the early 1970s.

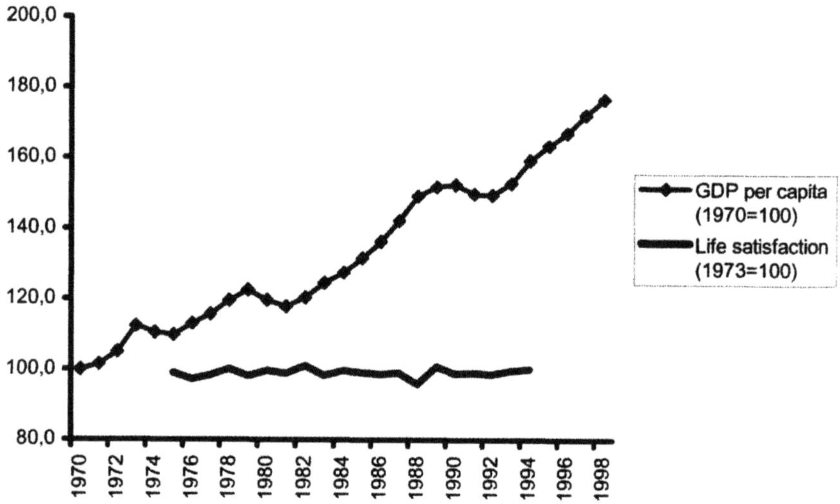

Figure 5: GDP and life satisfaction in the UK 1975 – 1996. While GDP per capita (1970: 100) has almost doubled, national mean life satisfaction (1973: 100) has remained almost the same. Source: Donovan et al. 2002: 17.

One interpretation of this paradox is based on the theory of innate needs: Once basic needs are met, there will be no increase in SWB from further gains of wealth (Diener/Suh 1999). The "threshold hypothesis" says that material growth only enhances people's well-being up to a certain point (Easterlin 1974, Max-Neef 1995, Veenhoven 1989). The degressive nature of the slope in the scatterplot in figure 4 would underline this assumption, pointing towards the law of decreasing marginal returns (Gossen 1854). A second point could be economic "bads" that have accompanied growth in these countries such as pollution and isolation[29] (Donovan et al. 2002, Durkheim 1893, Layard 2005, Offer 1996, 2006, Zolatas 1981). The third approach to this problem takes into account people's aspirations which may have grown at the same rate as the GNP in rich countries[30] (Easterlin 1995, 2001, Frey/Stutzer 2005, Inglehart 1990, Layard 2005, Offer 2006, Oswald 1997, Samuelson 1995). This notion is also referred to as the "satisfaction treadmill" (i.e. rising aspirations) or "hedonic treadmill" (i.e. habituation) (Brickman/Campbell 1971). The aspirations of people might also have shifted from material security to postmaterialist values, as Inglehart (1990) discovered. For the richer countries, the material indicator GDP would therefore lose explanatory power (Inglehart 1990, Delhey 2004). A fourth explanation to the paradox is the "positional treadmill", which indicates that along with one's income, the income of one's reference group, the "comparison others", has risen as well. But it is *relative* income that is important for life satisfaction rather than absolute income; this phenomenon was named "relative deprivation". Accordingly, the income of one's comparison other is assumed to have a negative effect on one's SWB if it is higher than one's own income (Blanchflower/Oswald

[29] Offer (1996: 8) therefore asks: "it is better to be rich than poor [...]. But it is no accident that the correlation [between income per capita and life satisfaction] falls well short of the perfect. What is the best use of affluence? And would further affluence be the highest priority?" Money would need to be spent on improving the quality of life of the individuals, rather than on the creation of more money. He thereby comes close to Nussbaum and Sen's suggestion (1993), that when looking at GDP as an indicator for QOL, one should sceptically ask whether the money is used to improve people's lives and how it is distributed.

[30] Higher income aspirations additionally reduce individual SWB (Diener et al. 1999, Nickerson et al. 2003, Stutzer 2004). In this respect, Layard (2005) reports that simply lowering one's aspirations in order to improve one's SWB does not work, though.

2000, Easterlin 1995, 2003, Helliwell 2001, Helliwell/Putnam 2004, Hirsch 1976, Kasser/Ryan 1993, Layard 2005, Michalos 1991, Oswald 1997)[31]. All in all, if we assume that everyday comparisons are made rather with one's neighbour than with people in another country, the economic approach may have more explanatory power at the individual level within nations rather than at the aggregate level across nations (Weller 1996).

Last but not least, the economic approach is problematic because a high GDP covaries with other factors that can increase SWB as well, like good health care, democratic political systems, human rights, increased consumption, individualism[32], etc. It is therefore difficult to disentangle which one of these factors is causing the higher SWB. The exact mechanisms and processes by which a high GDP increases SWB have therefore still not been fully explored (Diener/Suh 1999, Inglehart/Welzel 2005).

Inflation Rate and SWB

Besides the GNP, the inflation rate also serves as an indicator for economic security and well-being that was shown to correlate negatively with SWB in international comparisons. A high inflation rate usually signals economic volatility and uncertainty with negative effects on people's life satisfaction (Bjørnskov 2003, Di Tella et al. 2001, Frey/Stutzer 2002, Shafir et al. 1997, Shiller 1997).

[31] For further information on the role of social comparison for subjective well-being see Michalos' Multiple Discrepancies Theory (MDT) (1985, 2001); or Clark/Oswald (1996) Krause 2004, Neumark/Postlewaite (1998). Helliwell (2001: 55) described this phenomenon as "negative externalities" of income.

[32] Ahuvia (2001) argues that in rich countries, SWB values are higher not because of increased consumption, but because more individualistic cultures in rich nations encourage people to pursue personal happiness over meeting social obligations.

Unemployment Rate and SWB

The unemployment rate can be a third economic predictor for the national SWB score, since being unemployed lowers life satisfaction (Bjørnskov 2003, Clark/Oswald 1994, Gallie/Russel 1998, Helliwell/Putnam 2004, Keck/Delhey 2004, Mohr 1997)[33]. Unemployment has also negative effects beyond its monetary impact, like the breaking up of social networks (see also chapter 2.4) (Alesina/La Ferrara 2000, Bjørnskov 2003, Di Tella et al. 2001, Graham/Pettinato 2002, Helliwell 2001, Oswald 1997).

Income Equality and SWB

Income equality is similarly considered to increase SWB: first, by creating more social cohesion in a country when everybody has a similar social status. Second, it is likely that in a nation of equal opportunities, more individuals will have a perspective to reach their goals (Diener et al. 1995a, Veenhoven 1996a, Ouweneel/ Veenhoven 1991[34]). Of course, one could argue that nothing is won if everybody in a country is equally poor. However, if equality is high, there is less likelihood of negative externalities on one's SWB from the higher incomes of comparison others within a nation (Bjørnskov 2003, Helliwell 2001). Finally, many studies have found positive associations between income equality and average health status in the population, which additionally could enhance life satisfaction (Ben-Shlomo et al. 1996, Kawachi/ Kennedy 1999, Wilkinson 1996, Wolfson et al. 1999).

---

[33] Interestingly, being unemployed was shown to lower SWB to a higher degree in the 15 old EU member countries than in the new member states. This finding has been interpreted due to a bigger shadow economy in the new member states and because unemployment in those countries is more common (Keck/Delhey 2004).

[34] Ouweneel/Veenhoven (1991) found a correlation of $r = 0.40$ between income equality and SWB in nations. In a later study, though, they did not find an effect of income equality on SWB (Veenhoven/Ouweneel 1995, Veenhoven 1997).

To conclude, despite some problems the economic approach contains considerable plausibility and empirical support, especially in developing economies. Accordingly, the control variables GDP per capita, inflation, unemployment rate and income equality will be included in the subsequent multivariate regression analysis, in order to be able to identify the isolated effects of social capital on life satisfaction. However, the use of the economic approach as the standard explanation for differing national levels of SWB can be challenged on the basis of the criticism brought forward in this chapter. Instead, factors such as social capital need to be focussed upon.

2.3 Social Capital

The limitations of the economic approach in explaining international differences in SWB show that life is "more than a set of commercial relations" (Nussbaum/Sen 1993: 1). In addition, "virtually all researchers" have come to the conclusion that social relationships play a large role in determining life satisfaction (Donovan et al. 2002: 31, see also Argyle 1996, 1999, Myers 1999, Pugno 2005). In fact, supportive social relationships can even partly compensate for the hardship and poverty that people experience in an urban slum, as revealed by a study of slum dwellers in Calcutta, India (Biswas-Diener/Diener 2001). In essence, the basic idea behind the social capital approach highlights just that aspect: It is not so much money that makes people happy, but companionship, embodied as interpersonal trust and membership in networks (Lane 2000, Putnam 2000). The social capital approach with its emphasis on social embeddedness therefore seems to be very promising when trying to explain differing levels of SWB. Regarding the vast empirical evidence on social relationships and SWB, one can conclude that "the social nature of human beings is never more evident than when one reviews studies of subjective well-being" (Helliwell 2001: 55). At the aggregate level, too, the national mean SWB seems to be closely linked to the level of social capital in a country:

> "Societies differ in relation to the strength of their social ties, and this influences happiness independently of the individual's social relationships". It follows that "there are countries that simply create more happy people than other countries do and that the main difference between these countries lies in the social relationships" (Gundelach/Kreiner 2004: 383).

Based on these findings, the social capital approach was chosen to explain international differences in SWB by analysing the *effects of social capital on life satisfaction at the cross-national level* in the subsequent empirical study.

Definitions and Operationalisations of Social Capital

Since the 1990's, research on social capital and its effects on the "Well-being of Nations" (OECD 2001) has received numerous contributions from the social sciences. In the following chapter, the concept of social capital will be introduced. The notion of social capital that this book is based on was made popular by Robert Putnam in "Bowling Alone: The Collapse and Revival of American Community" (2000). According to his study on the declining social capital in the United States, social capital

> "refers to the collective value of all 'social networks' and the inclinations that arise from these networks to do things for each other" (Putnam 2000: 135).

It is operationalised as an index of the intensity of involvement in community and organisational life, public engagement, community and volunteering, informal sociability (e.g. visiting friends) and reported levels of interpersonal trust (Putnam 2000)[35]. Earlier, in a study on the political system in Italy, Putnam and colleagues (1993) had found social capital to be directly linked to democratic and economic development. In those regions where citizens participated more in associations, voted and read newspapers on a regular basis, the political and economic systems were more developed. The social capital in these regions was based on tight webs of social interaction which create an environment of social trust and low transaction costs in society. Accordingly, Putnam and colleagues defined social capital as follows:

> "social capital [...] refers to features of social organization, such as trust, norms, and networks that can improve the efficiency of society by facilitating coordinated actions" (Putnam et al. 1993: 167).

Later, Putnam and Helliwell (2004) added the precise effects of social networks to their definition:

> "social networks (and the associated norms of reciprocity and trust) can also have powerful effects on the level and efficiency of production and well-being, broadly defined, and [researchers] have used the term social capital to refer to these effects (Coleman 1988; Putnam 2000; OECD 2001; Woolcock 2001)" (Helliwell/Putnam 2004: 1436).

Although Putnam was the first scientist to study social capital at the level of the nation state or region (OECD 2001), his definition of the term is not the earliest one in the social sciences[36]. Instead, another

---

[35] Case studies of social capital in Great Britain, Sweden, Australia, Japan, France, Germany, Spain and the USA can be found in Putnam 2001.

[36] In fact, the idea of social capital can be traced to the work of Weber, Durkheim and de Tocqueville (OECD 2001). The first use of the actual term social capital

school of thought regarding social capital can be distinguished which is based on the works by Pierre Bourdieu (1986) and James Coleman (1988, 1990). It draws attention to the resources which individuals accumulate as a result of their membership of social networks. According to Coleman, who studied the role of social capital for the educational attainment of young people,

> "social capital is defined by its function. It is not a single entity, but a variety of different entities having two characteristics in common: They all consist of some aspect of social structure, and they facilitate certain actions of individuals who are within the structure. Like other forms of capital, social capital is productive, making possible the achievement of certain ends that would not be attainable in its absence" (Coleman 1990: 302).

Yet like in the case of Putnam, the mechanisms that generate social capital are networks of relationships, reciprocity, trust and social norms (Coleman 1988, 1990). In a similar fashion, Pierre Bourdieu defined social capital as "the aggregate of actual or potential resources which are linked to the possession of [...] membership in a group" (Bourdieu 1986: 249). In the end, this school of thought treats social capital as a feature that is invested in the individual. This could be considered the "network view" of social capital. On the other hand, there is Putnam's "communitarian view" of social capital, emphasising social cohesion. The latter considers social

---

goes back to Hanifan (1916) to describe rural school community centres. Moreover, it has been applied in classic works by Jacobs (1961), Loury (1977) and Granovetter (1982) (see also Fukuyama 2000, Adam/Roncevic 2004). However, only the two most influential schools of thought, namely Putnam vs. Coleman and Bourdieu (Portes 2000), shall be presented here. Out of the two, Putnam's definition will be used here, as explained below. (For an extensive account of the historical roots of the concept see Woolcock 1998.)

capital to be a social attribute that is inherent in the structure of social relationships and is both an ecological characteristic and a public good (Portes 2000, Yip et al. 2006). Since in this study SWB and social capital will be investigated at the societal level, the second perspective on social capital as expressed by Putnam seems to be more appropriate for the analysis. The societal dimension of social capital is the focus of attention in Putnam's theory. This is owed to the fact that Person A's civic engagement (e.g. sports club, church organisation etc.) is not only beneficial to himself, but also to Person B and everybody else in the community. In other words, Person A's social capital has "positive externalities" for Person B (Helliwell 2001: 55). An individual's social capital therefore raises the societal level of social capital. Exactly this societal level of social capital and its impact on national mean life satisfaction will be the central research interest of this analysis.

Even though Putnam's hypothesis, i.e. that social capital is declining in the United States, has been doubted due to contradicting data (Clark 1996, Fukuyama 2000, Gundelach/Kreiner 2004, Gundelach/Thorpe 1997, Ladd 1996, Schudson 1996), his work has sparked much subsequent research. Many sociologists have successively applied Putnam's operationalisation of social capital in either the original or a slightly modified form. For example, some studies picked organisational membership and participation in social networks as their indicator of social capital (e.g. Berkman/Syme 1979, Grootaert 2001, Gundelach/Kreiner 2004, Kawachi et al. 1997, 1999, Kennedy et al. 1998, Lochner et al. 2003, Ross/ Mirowsky 2002, Skrabski et al. 2004, Subramanian et al. 2001). Others measured social capital by interpersonal trust only (e.g. Brehm/Rahn 1997, Creed/Miles 1996, Ross et al. 2000, Woolcock 1998).

Nonetheless, most studies in the field of QOL research have operationalised social capital as both interpersonal trust and organisational membership (see for example Harpham et al. 2004, Helliwell 2003, 2006, Helliwell/Putnam 2004, Kennelly et al. 2003, Narayan/Pritchett 2000, Pollack/von dem Knesebeck 2004, Poortinga 2006, Rojas/Carlson 2005, von dem Knesebeck et al. 2005, World Bank 2004, Requena 2003 adding variables on commitment, communication and influence, Bjørnskov 2003 adding perceived corruption[37]).

A distinction has been introduced in the literature between *structural* social capital in terms of organisational membership, and *cognitive* social capital, which is measured by interpersonal trust (Harpham et al. 2002, Yip et al. 2006). Moreover, some scientists have suggested a third conceptual type, named *linking* social capital (Woolcock 1999, Woolcock/Narayan. 2000, World Bank 2000). This category refers to one's ties to authority, such as representatives of public (police, political parties) and private institutions.

A further distinction has sometimes been made between bonding social capital, i.e. networks, norms and understandings that facilitate cooperative activities within groups, and bridging social capital, which can exist between groups (Helliwell 2001, Narayan 2002,

---

[37] Narayan/Cassidy (2001) also consider corruption to be a major component of national social capital. A last, innovative way to operationalise social capital within a country has been suggested by Grjebine (2000). He studied to what extent people follow traffic rules, operationalised as the number of traffic fatalities, hypothesising that if people respect traffic rules within a country, the social consensus (and thus social capital) must be high. Many fatalities, like in the case of France, indicate low social capital and social trust. Few fatalities, like in Norway, mean that the social consensus to follow traffic rules is high, as is the level of social capital and people trust each other. Helliwell (2001: 39) empirically examined these assumptions and discovered in this respect that in OECD countries the variable interpersonal trust indeed explains more than one third of the variance of the number of traffic fatalities.

Putnam 2000). Accordingly, this study can be classified as focussing on bridging social capital only.

The role of social trust (i.e. the belief that others can be trusted) is twofold in social capital theory. While some researchers consider trust a part of the concept of social capital itself, others understand trust more as a result of social capital (Fukuyama 1995, Woolcock 2001), and use it as an indicator of the overall social capital in a society (Helliwell 2001). Hence, trust can be both a consequence as well as a facilitator of frequently used networks (Helliwell 2006). Either way, trust remains "a strong empirical index of social capital at the aggregate level" (Helliwell/Putnam 2004: 1436)[38].

On a final note, the concept of social capital seems to be of growing importance in sociology since its "breakthrough" with the works of Bourdieu, Coleman and Putnam (see Isham et al. 2002, who document the exponentially rising number of citations of social capital from 1993-2000). The concept of social capital is said to be undoubtedly one of the most noticeable recent "newcomers" in the social sciences. Since Putnam and colleagues' study (1993), "we are witnessing its unprecedented acceptance and application" (Adam/Roncevic 2004: 184). Today, many policy-making bodies and institutions have discovered its importance for well-being and development. The World Bank, for example, is developing its own "World Bank Social Capital Initiative":

> "To enhance its development effectiveness, the World Bank has, in recent years, taken an increasingly

---

[38] Finally, a related concept to social capital is Relational Wealth (RW) by Romesh Diwan (2000), according to whom human well-being consists of both material wealth and relational wealth. RW is defined as the harmoniousness of a society's relationships, especially to be able to live in harmony with one's environment.

> multidimensional approach to understanding the causes, manifestations, and consequences of poverty. In so doing, it has engaged in extensive conceptual, empirical and policy related work on social capital" (World Bank 2004: V).

In summary, social capital has become an important concept in the social sciences today. The next chapter will outline its links with research on SWB to provide a basis for the hypotheses.

2.4 The Theoretical Links from Social Capital to SWB

How does social capital enhance life satisfaction precisely? Figure 6 shows how the existing evidence and theoretical discussion in the literature has been structured to be presented in the following chapter. The six main mechanisms that embody the theoretical link will be outlined here. Empirical evidence to support the theoretical remarks will also be pointed out where appropriate.

As discussed at the beginning of chapter 2.3, a long tradition of research on SWB revealed that the quality of social relationships is one of the most important factors in predicting life satisfaction. Sometimes social relationships were ranked along with health but very often prior to income or education (Argyle 1999, Blanchflower/Oswald 2000, Donovan et al. 2002, Myers 1999).

In summary, many studies have revealed a positive effect of social capital on life satisfaction and other QOL indicators, controlling for other factors. Over and over again, people reported that good interpersonal relationships are prerequisites for their life satisfaction, often even more than money (Helliwell 2001, OECD 2001, Putnam 2000).

Structural Social Capital

1) *STRUCTURAL SOCIAL CAPITAL PROVIDES MORAL BACKING AND SOCIAL SUPPORT*

2) *STRUCTURAL SOCIAL CAPITAL EASES THE DISADVANTAGES OF MODERNISATION*

Cognitive Social Capital

3) *COGNITIVE SOCIAL CAPITAL BRINGS ABOUT LOW TRANSACTION COSTS AND LOWERS STRESS, THEREBY RAISING SWB*

Linking Social Capital

4) *LINKING SOCIAL CAPITAL PREVENTS PEOPLE FROM FEELING POWERLESS AND HELPLESS*

All Three Kinds of Social Capital

5) *SOCIAL CAPITAL FACILITATES ECONOMIC PROGRESS, GOOD HEALTH AND DEMOCRACY, WHICH ADDITIONALLY ENHANCE SWB*

6) *SOCIAL CAPITAL, AS AN ELEMENT OF SOCIAL COHESION, IMPROVES THE QOL IN A SOCIETY*

Figure 6: Summary of chapter 2.4 - the theoretical links at a glance.

Structural Social Capital

1) STRUCTURAL SOCIAL CAPITAL PROVIDES MORAL BACKING AND SOCIAL SUPPORT

First of all, networks provide social support. Structural social capital (i.e. membership or participation in associations) offers the members of a network social backing that enhances life satisfaction. It can be observed that:

> "People who have close friends and confidants, friendly neighbours and supportive co-workers are less likely to experience sadness, loneliness, low self-esteem and problems with eating and sleeping. Indeed, a common finding from research on the correlates of life satisfaction is that subjective well-being is best predicted by the breadth and depth of one's social connections. [...] Moreover, the 'happiness effects' of social capital in these various forms seem to be quite large, compared with the effects of material affluence" (Helliwell/Putnam 2004: 1437).

In countries with high social capital scores even economic shocks are compensated by this kind of social support because it reduces economic uncertainty (Rodrik 1999). Due to the positive externalities of social capital (see chapter 2.3), the whole society can benefit from the social capital of individuals. One's membership in a civic organisation (e.g. neighbourhood watch, sports association) is usually in some direct or indirect way beneficial to one's neighbours and fellow-citizens, too (Helliwell 2001). Environments of high social capital become environments with a high mean life satisfaction because people in them support each other:

> „What is at play in these countries is probably that social capital makes life easier and more predictable by removing small obstacles in everyday life while friends, families, colleagues and acquaintances can provide moral backing and behavioural outcomes of social capital may furthermore lead to people feeling a 'warm glow' of being trusted and having social interactions (Croson 1999)" (Bjørnskov 2003: 10).

Social capital thus leads to a better functioning society, both economically and politically, and environments with high levels of social capital may provide individuals with self-confidence and mutual assistance (OECD 2001). With regard to growing alienation, environments of high social capital where people are socially integrated through organisational membership, can offer effective backing and reduce stress (Bulmahn 2000, Veenstra 2000, Wilkinson 1996). Structural social capital can furthermore provide individuals with access to resources, which may in turn promote individual well-being. At the same time, social capital is a benefit at the community level that individuals can resort to in order to achieve collective goals that cannot be reached by individuals alone. For example, higher levels of social capital in the community may facilitate quicker and wider diffusion of ideas and important information (Yip et al. 2006).

Empirical Evidence

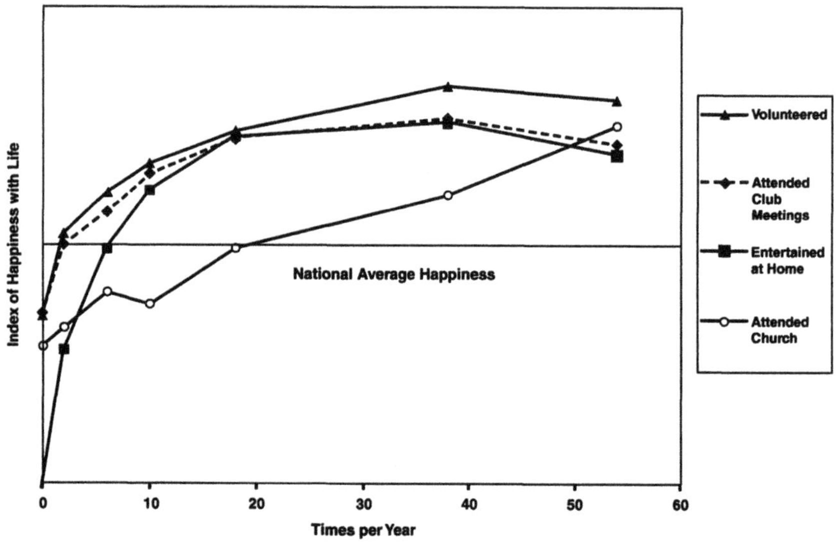

Figure 7: Social capital variables and happiness. Source: Putnam (2000): 334.

In his pilot study on social capital in the US, Putnam (2000) noted that social capital is associated with happiness at both individual and more aggregate levels. His social capital variables (involvement in community, public engagement, trust and informal sociability) were taken from the General Social Survey, the DDB Needham Life Style Survey, National Election Studies and the Roper Social and Political Trends Survey. They all correlated positively with SWB. The graph in figure 7 illustrates the positive association between (at least moderate levels of) the structural social capital variables of volunteering, attending club meetings and church services and receiving guests at home on the one hand, and an index of "happiness with life" on the other.

Similarly, Groot et al. (2006) found a significant effect of social capital on life satisfaction at the individual level. Their analysis of GPD survey data illustrate the sizeable income compensating effect of social capital, as measured by the size of the social network, the extent of the social safety net, and membership of a union or association. A positive correlation between structural social capital (organisational membership) and also cognitive social capital (a composite index of trust, reciprocity and mutual help) with SWB was confirmed by Yip et al. (2006). Their findings, drawn from their own sample of 1,218 interviewed people from rural China, revealed a positive effect of social capital on health. Likewise, in a study of work satisfaction in Spain, Requena (2003) reported the best predictor for SWB at the work place to be social capital. At the community level, stable neighbourhoods produce social capital in terms of profound horizontal ties and high levels of trust among its inhabitants and they were found to enhance the SWB of all neighbours (Ross et al. 2000). Finally, in their study involving 41 nations based on the WVS 1995-1997, Haller/Hadler (2004) reported that people who are participating actively in social and religious organisations are significantly happier than those who find themselves outside of such networks[39].

2) *Structural Social Capital Eases the Disadvantages of Modernisation*

A second theoretical link is based on the fact that the positive effects of being socially embedded help people to cope with the disadvantages of modernisation. This notion had already been outlined by modernisation theorists such as Emile Durkheim (1893). He reported the degree to which individuals are integrated into society to be closely linked to the incidence of suicide. The problem Durkheim describes is that individualisation brings about the replacement of close, often patrimonial ties in favour of anonymous, loose networks[40]. The falling apart of horizontal ties due to individualisation and modernisation has been named "anomie" (Degele/Dries 2005, Durkheim 1893). Under such conditions of low social capital, people lack a stable community base that provides support, identity and guidance. As a result, people experience cognitive dissonance and the rates of disaffection, suicide and violent crime increase across society (Durkheim 1893, Galtung 1996, Woolcock 1998).

Early modernisation theorists have inspired psychologists up to today, who indicate that individualisation may bring about "waning networks" (Myers 1999: 374, see also Kahnemann 1999). Less face-to-face contact apparently leads to alienation and declining trust. Consequences are a diminished sense of community, a loss of

---

[39] They also confirmed that both life satisfaction and happiness are higher in richer countries and in countries with a more equal distribution of income. Furthermore, in their study, life satisfaction was higher in well-developed welfare states and in politically free countries (Haller/Hadler 2004).

[40] This transformation has been described by Toennies in terms of "*Gemeinschaft*" and "*Gesellschaft*" (Toennies 2005).

purpose, thus finally depression and low SWB. Growing individualism in market societies makes people overlook the importance of social ties, whose "warmth of companionship" can lead to profound life satisfaction (Lane 2000: 110). In fact, the question whether human well-being will be ensured during on-going modernisation depends not least on the extent to which more effective mechanisms of social participation and integration will be developed in the future (Bulmahn 2000).

Cognitive Social Capital

3) Cognitive Social Capital Brings About Low Transaction Costs and Lowers Stress, thereby Raises SWB

A third mechanism by which social capital enhances life satisfaction assigns a central role to social trust, i.e. cognitive social capital:

> "Virtually all contemporary research on subjective well-being, quality of life, happiness and satisfaction with life as a whole shows that good interpersonal relations contribute more than anything else to these desirable states. If one were to list plausible necessary conditions for good interpersonal relations, trust would certainly be included in the list" (Michalos 1990: 619).

According to this logic, trust is a good indicator for the quality of social relationships. Where cognitive social capital (interpersonal trust) is high, social relationships must be in a good state. Environments of trust seem to play a central role in making people happy because in such an environment, individuals assume that others are "benevolent and do not rely on expensive safeguards or complicated contracts to support their economic and social ventures". That is to say that mistrust is a demanding state which requires "expensive protective baggage" and produces stress (Helliwell 2001: 47). Trust between individuals also lowers the transaction costs for the whole society (Fukuyama 1995, 2000) and most theoretical and empirical analysts agree that high levels of social trust make life "more enjoyable and more productive by reducing the costs of dealing with risk and uncertainty" (Helliwell 2001: 43).

A vivid illustration of the effects of high or low trust environments is the following anecdote, which can at the same time be supported by a strong empirical correlation. Danish mothers very often leave their baby trolleys (with the babies in them) outside shops and restaurants while they are inside. This habit famously led to a Danish mother being arrested in New York City, where this was considered inappropriate behaviour (New York Times 1997 as quoted in Zak/Knack 1998). So without conducting more advanced analyses yet, it can be stated at this point that Denmark is not only a country with a very high amount of interpersonal trust in many datasets (e.g. 66 per cent say that "most people can be trusted" in the 4th wave of the WVS). It is also ranks among the countries with the highest SWB in most studies (e.g. Bjørnskov 2003, Delhey 2004, Inglehart/Klingemann 2000, Weller 1996). On the other hand, a classic example for the effects of a lack of trust is the tribe of the Ik in Uganda, as described by Margaret Mead (in Woolcock 1998). In order to get even basic goods, the Ik were said to lie to and steal from everyone, including immediate family members. Not surprisingly, life in this "Hobbesian world was literally poor, nasty, brutish, and short" (Woolcock 1998: 172), and SWB would presumably be low (see more examples by Klitgaard 1990: 169).

Empirical Evidence

In an analysis based on over 83,000 cases from the WVS, plus the US Benchmark survey with over 28,000 cases and the Canadian ESC with 7,400 cases, a positive effect of social capital on SWB could be confirmed (Helliwell/Putnam 2004). The authors found each of their social capital variables (national percentage of generalised trust, trust in police and neighbours and average membership in associations) to correlate positively with both happiness and life satisfaction items. Especially cognitive social capital was associated positively with SWB so that individuals who reported themselves as living in a high-trust environment also had significantly higher levels of SWB. In summary, being able to trust others - both those among whom one lives and those in authority - was strongly associated with higher levels of life satisfaction and of happiness (Helliwell/Putnam 2004). Cognitive social capital was also reported to correlate with life satisfaction in studies by Freitag (2003), Inglehart (1990) and Rotter (1980). The latter, for example, revealed a positive association between trust and SWB in an analysis of university students.

Linking Social Capital

4) Linking Social Capital Prevents People from Feeling Powerless and Helpless

Confidence and trust have always been necessary conditions of people living together in communities (Sellerberg 1982). Society is possible only through trust in its members (i.e. cognitive social capital) and trust in its institutions (i.e. linking social capital) (Lewis/Weigert 1985). With regard to linking social capital, as a fourth theoretical mechanism by which social capital enhances SWB, psychologists claim that people feel powerless, helpless and in consequence alienated, if citizens' trust in the institutions is low (Frey/Stutzer 2002). After all, cognitive and linking social capital particularly enhance life satisfaction because people find their social context to be so important. They "value trust in their neighbourhoods, their workplaces, their public services and their public servants" (Helliwell 2006: 43).

Empirical Evidence
Focussing on linking social capital, Veenhoven (1993) discovered that the correlation between political trust and average happiness was rather high in Europe – although it was lower for the rest of the world. He hypothesised that people expect their governments and institutions to act in their interest, while the citizens' life satisfaction decreases if that does not seem to be the case.

All Three Kinds of Social Capital

5) SOCIAL CAPITAL FACILITATES ECONOMIC PROGRESS, GOOD HEALTH AND DEMOCRACY, WHICH ADDITIONALLY ENHANCE SWB

A fifth theoretical linkage is the fact that social capital has positive effects on mediating variables like health, economic progress and democracy. The direct linkages running from social capital to SWB may be better documented in the literature and are likely to be of greater theoretical and empirical significance (Helliwell 2001). Nonetheless, the benefits of social capital for SWB through these third variables should be noted. At the level of the neighbourhood, social capital may increase health through the diffusion of health information, through health promoting norms, high levels of social control, lower crime rates, and access to services and amenities. Aggregating to the level of the state or nation, social capital may lead to better government functioning and healthcare delivery (von dem Knesebeck et al. 2005). Furthermore, a social network may increase the subjective life expectancy of a person by creating assurance about the future, by reinforcing healthy habits, by improving current health and in a last consequence the person's SWB (Ross/Mirowsky 2002).

Concerning another mediating variable between social capital and SWB, economic progress, it has been found that especially trust facilitates economic growth. Figuratively speaking, "trust acts like a lubricant that makes any group or organization run more efficiently" (Fukuyama 2000: 98). The economic development resulting from high trust environments brings about an economic optimism which then influences overall life satisfaction (Fukuyama 1995, Knack/Keefer 1997, Temple 2000, Zak/Knack 1998). Countries with high levels of social capital also tend to be more democratic and more egalitarian. All in all, they are in many ways more liveable than societies with low social capital because where certain individuals are engaged in civic life, the social capital they produce has positive effects for the whole society (Putnam 2000).

Empirical Evidence

Many studies revealed social capital to be positively associated to other QOL variables, such as health, which may then eventually enhance life satisfaction (e.g. Berkman/Glass 2000, Kawachi et al. 1997, Kawachi et al. 1999, Kawachi/Berkman 2003, Lindström 2004, Lochner et al. 2003, Pollack/von dem Knesebeck 2004, Poortinga 2005, Skrabski et al. 2004, Subramanian et al. 2001). For example, von dem Knesebeck et al. (2005) reported significant correlations in 21 European countries at both individual and country levels. Controlling for GDP and other factors, countries with low levels of social capital had a high percentage of citizens reporting poor health. The bivariate association between the average number of memberships in organisations per person in a country and the percentage of residents reporting fair or poor health, for example, was $r = -0.72$ ($p < 0.01$). The correlation between social trust and fair or poor health was $r = -0.70$ ($p < 0.01$). Other studies in this field linked social capital, as aggregated to the collective level, to lower overall mortality rates (Berkman/Syme 1979, Rojas/Carlson 2005), lower violent crime rates (Kennedy et al. 1998), lower tuberculosis rates (Holtgrave/ Crosby 2004), higher subjective life expectancy (Ross/Mirowsky 2002) and lower suicide rates (Helliwell 2004). No significant correlation between social capital and health indicators was observed by Veenstra (2000), Kennelly et al. (2003), and Harpham et al. (2004). Social capital was finally also reported to increase human capital and thus SWB through this mediating variable (OECD 2001, Schuller 2002).

6) SOCIAL CAPITAL, AS AN ELEMENT OF SOCIAL COHESION, IMPROVES THE QOL IN A SOCIETY

Last but not least, social capital is part of the concept of social cohesion. Social cohesion is twofold: one dimension describes the absence of social disparities, inequalities, fragmentations and cleavages. The other dimension focuses on strengthening social relations and ties within a society; in other words - social capital. Social cohesion in this respect enhances the QOL in a society because citizens can relate to one another. Subsequently, social cohesion has been declared a major policy goal for instance by the EU (2000) [41].

Empirical Studies as Role-Models for this Analysis

Looking at the cross-national level, Helliwell/Putnam (2004: 1443) concluded that those "nations with higher membership densities show higher average levels of life satisfaction". Likewise, Helliwell (2003) noted that variations in national trust levels over time and across countries have a large and significant effect on SWB. He conducted a study of 50 nations using data from three waves of the WVS. Gundelach/Kreiner (2004) also studied the effects of structural social capital on SWB at the cross-national level. They reported that "social capital is the most important predictor of

[41] Further countries and institutions that have also recently investigated how to improve social cohesion in their regions include the OECD, European Commission, Council of Europe and the governments of France, Canada and the Netherlands (Berger-Schmitt 2002, Berger-Schmitt/Noll 2000).

happiness at the aggregate level" (ibid.: 383). Their analysis was based on the European Values Survey and included nine countries.

The first ones to note a correlation between societies with high SWB and high values of interpersonal trust, however, were Inglehart/Rabier (1984a, 1984b, 1986). In their study entitled "Why are the Belgians so much happier than the French?" (1986) they reject the economic approach and linguistic arguments to explain international differences in SWB as insufficient. Instead, they argue that interpersonal trust was better suited as a reason for why some countries have higher national mean life satisfaction scores than others. In a related article, they concluded that countries which rank high in SWB very often have superior levels of social trust, too:

> „Les pays qui se caractérisent par un niveau élevé de bien-être subjectif ont, en effet, une tendence marquée à occuper une bonne place sur le plan de la confiance accordée à autrui. [..] La confiance à l'égard d'autrui et le bien-être subjectif ont une certaine propension à aller de pair" (Inglehart/Rabier 1984 : 25).

Their study of 11 countries based on the 1981 WVS stops with this observation and unfortunately did not explore social capital as explanatory variable any further. Another more detailed, multivariate analysis was conducted by Bjørnskov (2003), who noted a correlation of SWB and the social capital variables generalised trust, civic participation and perceived corruption. Including national mean values of 32 countries from the 4th wave of the WVS in his regression analysis, he concluded that:

> "at the national level, social capital indeed seems to lead to happiness over and above its effects on income and uncertainty. While the paper corroborates the previous findings that income, economic stability, future prospects and certain other features influence

> people's life satisfaction, the relationship between social capital and happiness emerges as strong and remarkably robust to testing for a set of supplementary ideas" (Bjørnskov 2003: 14).

The bivariate association between national mean social capital and SWB was high ($r = 0.75$) and strongly significant. Controlling for GNI, inflation and income inequality, the effects of social capital remained prominent and significant with a beta value of $\beta = 0.47$ and $p < 0.01$.

3. Hypotheses

Main Hypotheses

The theoretical explanations of chapter 2.4, together with the broad empirical support, ultimately lead to the following hypotheses. The main hypothesis of this book will be that there is a positive effect of social capital variables on life satisfaction scores (at the cross-national level). Such a positive correlation has been observed by various researchers using different data sets. The association is based on the assumption that having social capital, or even simply living in an environment with a lot of social capital (due to its positive externalities), will enhance people's life satisfaction through the various mechanisms outlined in the previous section. Different social capital variables will be used in the analysis. Complying with previous research, *cognitive* social capital (interpersonal trust), *structural* social capital (membership and participation in associations) and *linking* social capital (trust in authority and institutions) will be distinguished. Consequently, the hypotheses are:

H1: The more *cognitive* social capital (x_1) there is in a country, the higher the nation's mean life satisfaction score will be.

H2: The more *structural* social capital (x_2) there is in a country, the higher the nation's mean life satisfaction score will be.

H3: The more *linking* social capital (x_3) there is in a country, the higher the nation's mean life satisfaction score will be.

Rich vs. Poor and Middle-Income Countries

Next to the basic analysis for the whole sample, an additional analysis of rich and poor[42] nations separately seems promising: Because as previous cross-national studies suggest (see for example Easterlin 1974, Inglehart/Klingemann 2000, chapter 2.2), the effects of economic factors on SWB tend to diminish above a threshold of 13,000 US-$ GDP per capita/year. Consequently, it can be assumed for this study, too, that economic factors such as GDP will lose explanatory power for national mean life satisfaction in wealthy nations, while a non-economic factor such as social capital will then be more prominent. Accordingly, economic factors would be more important than social capital in the poor nations. Following this logic, the effect of economic factors on national mean life satisfaction would be more visible in poor nations than in rich countries, while the reverse would be true for social capital. These assumptions can be formulated as follows.

H4:	The importance of the effect of *social capital* on national mean life satisfaction will be *higher* in rich countries than in poor countries.
H5:	The importance of the effect of *GDP* on national mean life satisfaction will be *lower* in rich countries than in poor countries.
H6:	In *rich* countries, the effect of *social capital* on life satisfaction will be more important than the effect of GDP.
H7:	In *poor countries*, the effect of *GDP* on life satisfaction will be more important than the effect of social capital.

[42] The expressions "poor" and "poor and middle-income" will be used synonymously when describing the country sample in the following chapters.

Hypotheses 4 to 7 can be visualised in a simple 2x2 matrix as in table 3. The table displays which standardised coefficient scores can be expected in comparison to each other when later running separate analyses for rich and poor nations.

Table 3: The Hypothesised Relative Importance of the Effect of Social Capital vs. GDP on National Mean Life Satisfaction in Rich vs. Poor Countries

Importance of the effect of...	in rich countries	in poor countries
...social capital	++	+
...GDP	+	++

++ = relatively larger beta value expected; + = relatively smaller beta value expected

Control Variables

The hypotheses for the control variables also result directly from the theoretical remarks and prior empirical findings as presented and discussed in chapter 2.2.

H8: The higher a country's *GDP per capita*, the higher the nation's mean life satisfaction score will be.

H9: The more *income equality* (as measured by the Gini coefficient) there is in a country, the higher the nation's mean life satisfaction score will be.

H10: The lower a country's *inflation* rate, the higher the nation's mean life satisfaction score will be.

H11: The lower the *unemployment* rate in a country, the higher the nation's mean life satisfaction score will be.

Path Diagram

The framework of the analysis is illustrated in figure 8. As described earlier, hypotheses H1 to H3 assume a positive association between the social capital variables and national mean life satisfaction. Hypotheses H8 and H9 predict a positive association for the control variables GDP and income equality, while H10 and H11 forecast negative associations for inflation and unemployment rates. To test H4 to H7, the analysis as outlined in figure 8 will be run for rich and poor countries individually, in addition to the first general analysis including all countries.

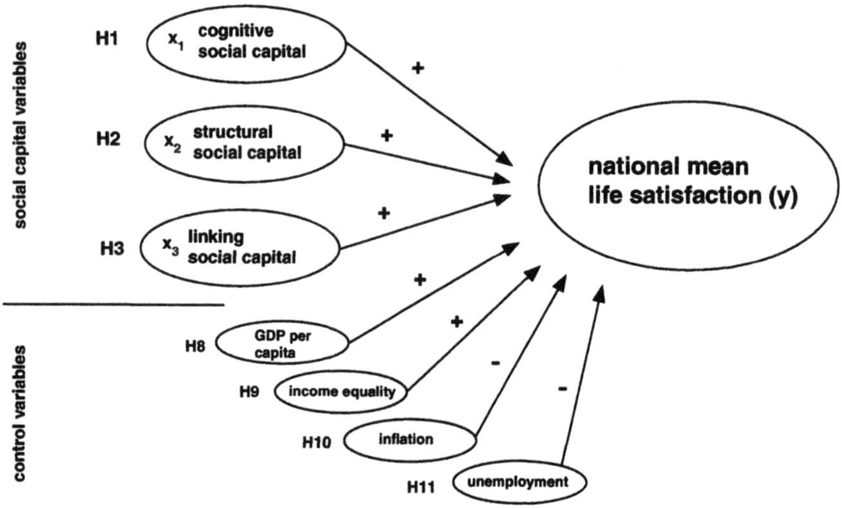

Figure 8: Path diagram.

4. Operationalisation

The following operationalisations were chosen in order to closely parallel previous research on this issue (see chapter 2.3). To perform a national level analysis, individual scores from the dataset were aggregated, so that each score represents a country in a certain survey year (e.g. Slovenia 1995).

4.1 Life Satisfaction

Life Satisfaction will be measured in terms of generalised life satisfaction for the reasons outlined in chapter 2.1.4. In the WVS, respondents were asked: "All things considered, how satisfied are you with your life as a whole these days? Using this card on which 1 means you are 'completely dissatisfied' and 10 means you are 'completely satisfied' where would you put your satisfaction with your life as a whole?" Answers are consequently represented on a metric variable with a range from 1 to 10.

4.2 Cognitive Social Capital

Cognitive social capital is usually measured in terms social trust (see chapter 2.3). The WVS contains questions about specific trust in certain groups (e.g. racial groups, neighbours, family), as well as a generalised trust question. In this study, generalised trust will be used, i.e. respondent's answers to the question: "Generally speaking, would you say that most people can be trusted or that you need to be very careful in dealing with people?" In order to compare scores cross-nationally, the nominal variable with two answer options was aggregated and transformed into a metric variable containing national percentages of respondents who said that "most people can be trusted" (see for example Helliwell/ Putnam 2004).

The generalised trust question was chosen for various reasons: The canonical question has been used in surveys since Almond and Verba (1963) as a standard assessment of social trust and it is asked in all survey waves of the WVS. Previous research revealed that the generalised trust question also has the highest test-retest reliability compared to other variables of social trust, such as trust in friends, neighbours etc. Moreover, correlations of the generalised question are high with specific trust items, and answers to the generalised question from various cities correlated with the frequency with which deliberately "lost" wallets were returned in an experiment[43] (Knack/Keefer 1997). Furthermore, the canonical question was shown not to suffer from translation problems in cross-national surveys. Finally, the term "most people" is interpreted by the majority of respondents as fellow citizens of one's own nation, which makes the generalised trust variable very suitable for a cross-national analysis (Helliwell 2001, Helliwell/Putnam 2004, Knack 2001, Knack/Keefer 1997).

4.3 Structural Social Capital

Structural social capital is defined as membership and participation in associations in the literature (see chapter 2.3). In this study it is thus operationalised as the number of types of associations that

[43] In this experiment, wallets (with an address inside) were deliberately left in random streets of various cities. The number of returned wallets indeed corresponded to survey results enquiring about generalised trust in those cities (the correlation being r = 0.65) (Knack/Keefer 1997).

respondents are an inactive or an active member of. For this purpose, the many nominal variables of the survey were transformed into two metric ones: The original question in the survey was "Now I am going to read off a list of voluntary organizations. For each one, could you tell me whether you are an active member, an inactive member or not a member of that type of organization?"[44] with the answer options "yes" or "no". Examples of types of associations are environmental organisations, political parties or sports associations. Out of those single nominal variables, a new metric variable for inactive membership on the one hand ("sum_inactive"), and one for active participation on the other hand ("sum_active") were created, each capturing the *number* of the types of associations that respondents are involved in. The potential maximum is 8 types of associations[45]. A third variable sums up active and inactive memberships ("sum_memberships") with a potential maximum of 16 types of associations. The latter variable will be used in the regression analysis as the broadest and most commonly used indicator of structural social capital (as reported in chapter 2.3).

[44] In a similar fashion, the 1st, 2nd and 3rd wave of the WVS asked about inactive memberships by saying: "Please look carefully at the following list of voluntary organisations and activities and say which, if any, do you belong to?" And they enquired about active memberships by asking: "And for which, if any, are you currently doing unpaid voluntary work?" Membership scores from all WVS waves are included in the two new metric variables.

[45] This applies to the 4th wave of the WVS. In the 1st, 2nd and 3rd wave, 14 types of associations were offered to respondents to choose from. The empirically observed range is from 0.03 to 2.82 types of associations for active memberships and 0.08 to 3.24 for inactive memberships (national averages). Combining the different scales of all waves is still feasible since 91.5 per cent of cases have an average membership rate below 3 types of associations anyways, and the maximum score is below 6, too (see chapter 6).

4.4 Linking Social Capital

Linking social capital is defined as the people's ties to authority and is operationalised as trust in various state institutions. Certain variables from the WVS cover this topic. Respondents were asked: "I am going to name a number of organizations. For each one, could you tell me how much confidence you have in them: is it a great deal of confidence, quite a lot of confidence, not very much confidence or none at all?" Answers are collected on an interval scale ranging from 1 to 4 which were recoded so that high scores indicate a lot of confidence, in order to better illustrate positive relationships in the regression analysis later. Furthermore, to get a good indicator with a broad range of institutions, an index "confidence in institutions" consisting of various variables was created. The most suitable variables were people's confidence in the armed forces, police, parliament and civil services.

Table 4: Descriptive Statistics of the Variables in the Index Variable "Confidence in Institutions" (Linking Social Capital)

N = 152	Confidence in armed forces	Confidence in police	Confidence in parliament	Confidence in civil services
Mean	2.70	2.58	2.31	2.40
St.dev.	0.36	0.36	0.34	0.28

Score of 1 = no confidence in the organisation; 4 = a great deal of confidence in the organisation.

Ensuring the Quality of the Index

These items were chosen because they represent various components of "authority". But moreover, using these four variables the highest empirical consistency can be reached, that is to say they come closest to measuring the same thing. The quality of the index was tested by measuring the correlation between the new index variable "confidence in institutions" and each individual item that it consists of. Their respective correlation score with the index variable is sufficiently high. The quality of each variable is indicated by a high r score.

Table 5: Correlation between Index Variable "Confidence in Institutions" and the Variables that it Consists of

N = 152	Confidence in armed forces	Confidence in police	Confidence in parliament	Confidence in civil services
r score	0.68	0.73	0.83	0.82

The r scores of the four variables can be considered sufficient, although they should ideally all be above 0.8. Other items dealing with trust in institutions that were tested, e.g. "confidence in press", had to be excluded because of a too low r score (0.57). On the index variable, too, a low score of 1 indicates little trust in authority (little linking social capital), while a high score of 4 stands for much confidence in the institutions (much linking social capital).

4.5 Control Variables

Chapter 2.2 discussed which control variables will be worth including in the empirical analysis. The following economic factors will be considered in the study.

GDP is a widely used measure for material wealth in a society. It is defined as the market value of all final goods and services produced within a country in a given period of time (Black 2003). To allow for international comparisons, it will be indicated per capita and per year, adjusted to power-purchasing-parity. The scores in US-Dollars were recoded into steps of 1000 US-Dollars for the regression and will enter the analysis as a metric variable.

Income equality is represented by the Gini coefficient, which is a mathematical measure of the inequality of a distribution. It enters the regression as a metric variable with a potential range from 0 (maximum equality) to 100 (maximum inequality).

The inflation rate is the rate of increase (or decrease) of the average price level in a country that indicates economic volatility. It is measured in per cent and will be included in the analysis as a metric variable. Scores can be negative (decrease of price level) or positive (increase of price level).

The unemployment rate will be indicated in per cent, representing the number of unemployed workers divided by the total civilian labour force of a nation. The unemployment rate will therefore be included in the regression as a metric variable.

5. Data and Method

The data that this study is based on is taken from all four waves of the World Values Survey (WVS) including data from the European Values Survey (EVS)[46]. The WVS data have become increasingly well-known in recent years, and have been utilised in hundreds of publications in more than twenty languages. The Surveys grew out of a study launched by the European Values Survey group under the leadership of Jan Kerkhofs and Ruud de Moor in 1981. With more than 80 countries having been surveyed in total, these countries represent almost 85 per cent of the world's population. The WVS therefore provides a fairly unique data base of the values and beliefs of mass publics on political and social life (World Values Survey Group 2006). The advantages of using the WVS in this study lie in its vast global coverage, plus the availability of many waves from different years and in the fact that it provides both life satisfaction as well as social capital variables. A disadvantage could be the fact that the survey is conducted in one standardised version for all countries and does not take into account cultural differences.

I will conduct an analysis of pooled data from all survey waves in order to increase the number of cases. Survey waves were carried out in 1981, 1990-1991, 1995-1996 and 1999-2001. After aggregating the data to the national level there were 210 observations. Each observation represents a country in a certain

---

46 Data file (.sav) taken from www.worldvaluessurvey.org, accessed on 12 October 2006. EUROPEAN AND WORLD VALUES SURVEYS FOUR-WAVE INTEGRATED DATA FILE, 1981-2004, v.20060423, 2006. The European Values Study Foundation and World Values Survey Association. Aggregate File Producers: ASEP/JDS, Madrid, Spain/Tilburg University, Tilburg, the Netherlands. Aggregate File Distributors: ASEP/JDS and ZA, Cologne, Germany.

year, whereas 152 cases provided the social capital variables necessary for the subsequent analysis. All in all, these 152 observations sum up the answers of 181,574 respondents at the aggregate level. The scores of certain control variables were not available for some countries, though. Once control variables enter the multivariate regression analysis, the number of observations will consequently be reduced to the 125 cases for which scores on all variables could be obtained. This reduction of cases does not distort the results, though, as the descriptive statistics of the 152 cases (see chapter 6) are widely identical with those of the 125 cases (see appendix). The sample will be split up in an additional analysis into two sub-samples of rich countries on the one hand, and poor and middle-income countries on the other hand. In line with the literature (Inglehart/Klingemann 2000), countries above a threshold of 13,000 US-$ GDP per capita/year will be classified as rich. A risk of autocollinearity shall be mentioned here, since the 152 cases do not stand for 152 different countries but 72, whereas some are surveyed at several points in time[47]. Consequently, the Durbin-Watson coefficient will be checked in the regression analysis.

The scores of the control variables GDP per capita, inflation rate and unemployment rate are taken from the World Bank (2006): *World Development Indicators (CD-ROM)*. The Gini coefficients can be found in UNU-WIDER (2005)[48].

Since all the variables are metric, it will be appropriate to use ordinary least square (OLS) regression. Following bivariate analyses for each type of social capital, a multivariate regression analysis will be conducted.

---

[47] However, in the following chapters the expressions "cases" and "countries" will be used synonymously to allow for fluent reading.

[48] http://www.wider.unu.edu/wiid/wiid.htm; accessed on 16 April 2007.

Challenges of a Cross-National Analysis

There are some methodological problems involved when comparing data gathered in different nations and cultures that should be discussed here. Issues that can arise concern construct equivalence, administration, format, response style, the tendency to guess, and the social desirability factor. Finally, peoples' cultural backgrounds affect to what extent they are accustomed to answering attitudinal or self-rating questions (Frey/Stutzer 2002, Hudler/Richter 2002, Hambleton/Patsula 1998, Utsey et al. 2001). Another major problem when making quantitative cross-national comparisons has always been the small number of countries (cases) that the studies consist of. However, "time is gradually solving this problem" (Helliwell 2006: 39) as more and more countries are covered by surveys. In the following analysis, for example, scores for 74 different countries (152 cases in total) from the WVS could be considered.

Some cultural critics argue that SWB research was grounded in the western notion that happiness is the ultimate goal in life. While the concept has strong psychometric properties in industrialised western societies, it would accordingly be an ethnocentristic idea that does not produce valid results in other cultures (Diener/Suh 2000, Lyubomirsky/Lepper 1999, Segall et al. 1990, Veenhoven 1996b, Vittersø et al. 2002). Indeed, there is a debate in QOL research about the problem of "cultural relativism", focussing on the question whose standards should be used when assessing the quality of life. While many social researchers claim that there are universal standards for the quality of life (see for example Nussbaum/Sen 1993, H. Putnam 1993, Scanlon 1993, Nussbaum 1993, Taylor 1993), others see the need to take into account the respective local standards of each cultural group, in particular with respect to the distinction between individualist and collectivist cultures (see for example Diener/Oishi 2000, 2004, Kitayama/Markus 2000, Oishi 2000, Oishi et al. 1999, Suh 2000, Suh et al. 1998, Triandis 2000,

Utsey et al. 2001, Walzer 1993). Latter, relativist approaches take into account the different philosophies of happiness in different parts of the world. While, for example, western mainstream philosophy encourages the individual to pursue self-fulfilment, Confucian thinking argues for order and harmony of the whole society (Diener/Suh 2000, Tiberius 2004). On the other hand, the universalist approach suggests that life satisfaction scores are comparable across nations. There is a danger of simplifying those possible differences in philosophies when research on life satisfaction is conducted in various cultures with the same method of data collection. However, this approach is the only way to make large, quantitative comparisons of different groups and regions (next to qualitative methods with much fewer cases). Moreover, empirical research has shown that life satisfaction indeed is a concept with cross-cultural generality (Bargatzky 2002, Frey/Stutzer 2002, Ouweneel/Veenhoven 1991, Rapley 2003, Vittersø et al. 2002).

A second question when making cross-national comparisons is whether nations are meaningful units of analysis, seeing as some countries are very heterogeneous and there are huge differences between people within countries. Nonetheless, the empirical evidence says that they are. First of all, the relative rankings of countries in terms of their mean SWB scores are quite stable over time (Inglehart/Klingemann 2000). That is to say that the international differences in SWB are not arbitrary, also because the correlate with other QOL indicators such as suicide rates (Helliwell 2004, 2006, Helliwell/Putnam 2004). Moreover, different cross-national surveys deliver highly consistent scores for nations. Diener et al. (1995) found an average Pearson's correlation of r = 0.71 between the national mean levels of SWB in three different cross-national surveys. Second, there is also consistency within nations, given the fact that comparing various sub-groupings across nations delivers a homogenous picture. For example, the national means for men are almost perfectly predictable from the scores for women (with a correlation of r = 0.97; the correlation between the different age groups within a nation for instance is r = 0.93). That is to say that there is a high degree of homogeneity of SWB within nations (Diener/Suh 1999). Numerous scholars therefore argue that subjective measures ought to be used in cross-national comparisons (e.g. Frey/Stutzer 2002, Vittersø et al. 2002).

After all, it seems to be a very interesting challenge in the research on life satisfaction to explain why there are such large and considerably stable differences in the national means. Some societies seem to provide better living conditions for their citizens than others (Gundelach/Kreiner 2004). This analysis will be dedicated to that question, too, whilst not overlooking the methodological problems mentioned here.

6. Descriptive Statistics

Table 6: Descriptive Statistics of the Dependent and the Independent Variables for all Countries in the Sample

variable	all countries (n = 152)		
	mean of all nations	**standard deviation**	**range**
dependent variable:			
(y) life satisfaction, national means	6.71	1.11	3.73 – 8.49
independent variables:			
(x_1) cognitive social capital: generalised trust, national percentages	32.91	12.88	13.7 – 66.1
(x_2) structural social capital: membership, national means	1.63	1.00	0.11 – 5.86
(x2a) structural social capital: *active* membership, national means	0.61	0.47	0.03 – 2.82
(x2b) structural social capital: *inactive* membership, national means	1.02	0.64	0.08 – 3.24
(x3) linking social capital: index trust in institutions, national means	2.50	0.26	1.91 – 3.49

Table 6 displays important descriptive statistics for the sample of 152 observations[49]. The differences in national mean life satisfaction between the countries are quite considerable, ranging between 3.73 and 8.49. Life satisfaction is highest in Puerto Rico (2001), Colombia (1998), Malta (1991) and Denmark (1991). Cases at the bottom of the table are the Republic of Moldova (1996), Zimbabwe (2001), Ukraine (1996) and the Russian Federation (1995)[50].

The cross-national variation in generalised trust is remarkable, too, since the percentage of people in a country who think that "most people can be trusted" varies from 13.7 per cent to 66.1 per cent in the WVS sample. Furthermore, average membership in types of associations across nations seems quite low, since the mean value of all countries is (active and inactive) membership in 1.63 types of associations per person. Last but not least, trust in the institutions varies less within the sample, as the low standard deviation and the small range of observed scores indicate.

Table 7 shows the descriptive statistics of the control variables. The datasets provide the scores for 125 cases on all the control variables. Rich countries, such as Luxembourg (1999) and the United States (1999), as well as poor countries like Nigeria (1995) and Bangladesh (1996) are included in the sample. The overall mean of the Gini coefficient is with 35.51 closer to 0 (maximum equality) than to 100 (maximum inequality). Nations with a fairly unequal distribution of incomes will be studied (e.g. South Africa 2001, Chile 2000), along

[49] The 152 cases described in table 6 will be included in the bivariate analyses. For a table featuring the descriptive statistics of the 125 cases used in the multivariate analysis see appendix; the differences are minimal, though. Descriptive statistics of the rich and poor subgroups separately can also be found in the appendix, where they are compared.

[50] For a detailed overview of the national mean life satisfaction scores for each country and survey year see appendix.

with more egalitarian nations (e.g. China 1990, Slovakia 1991). In the case of inflation, two outliers were excluded, so that the mean inflation is now 24.54 per cent. Mean unemployment in the sample is moderate at 9.28 per cent. Nonetheless, the range is from near full employment (Sweden 1990) to almost a third of the labour force being without a job (Republic of Macedonia 1998).

Table 7: Descriptive Statistics of the Control Variables for all Countries

variable	**all countries (n = 125)**		
	mean of all nations	**standard deviation**	**range**
control variables:			
GDP per capita, US-$	12,141	8,642	779 – 48,730
gini coefficient	35.51	10.41	18.0 – 60.1
inflation, per cent	24.54	70.43	-1.17 – 555.38
unemployment rate, per cent	9.28	5.93	1.80 – 32.40

7. Analysis and Interpretation of Results

7.1 All Countries: In Summary a Considerable Effect of Social Capital

7.1.1 Bivariate Analysis

Each type of social capital and its relationship with life satisfaction will be examined in a scatterplot, before conducting the multivariate regression analysis. The following curve estimations each produce the respective best fit line according to the least squares criterion. This is the line for which the sum of squared deviations is least (Brosius 2006).

Cognitive Social Capital and Life Satisfaction
The bivariate analysis in figure 9 and the correlation coefficient $r = 0.34$ ($p = 0.00$) indicate a linear, significant, positive, moderate association between cognitive social capital and life satisfaction. This correlation for the 152 cases in the study supports hypothesis 1, according to which the more cognitive social capital there is in a society, the higher the nation's mean life satisfaction score will be. The regression equation here is $y = 5.8 + 0.03 \cdot x$. The equation specifies that - starting at a life satisfaction score of 5.8 if there is no trust at all within a society - for every per cent increase of people who say that "most people can be trusted", a nation's mean life satisfaction score rises by 0.03 points. The overall explanatory power of this model, however, is not very high as indicated by the value of R square = 0.12. In other words, only 12 per cent of the variance of the dependent variable can be explained by the independent variable. This is in part owed to the bivariate nature of the model, and the multivariate regression analysis in chapter 7.1.2

will presumably bring forward models with higher values for the adjusted R square.

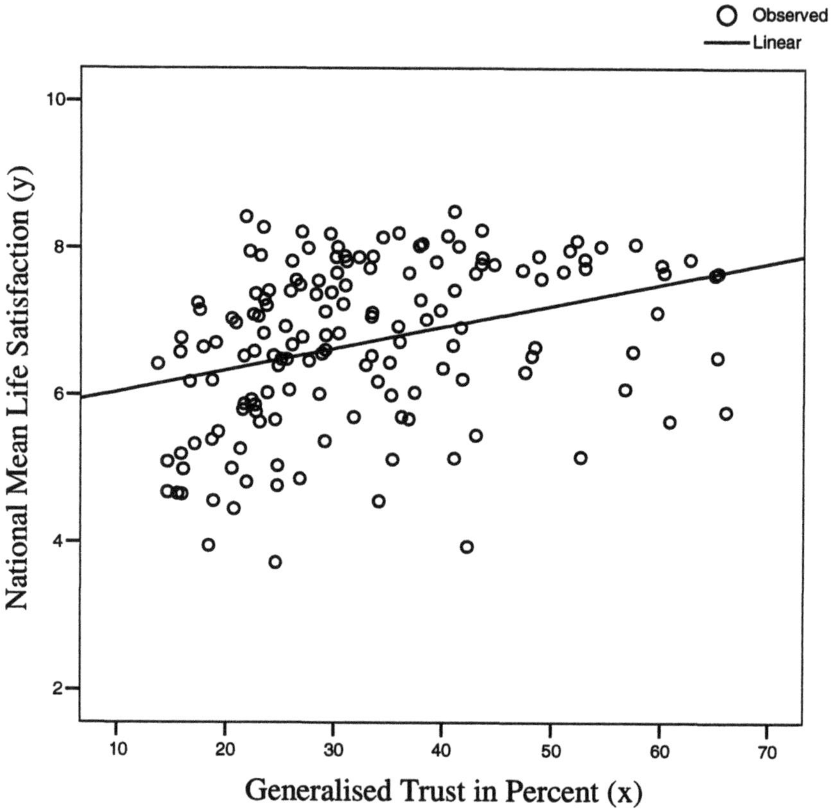

Figure 9: National mean life satisfaction (y) and generalised trust (cognitive social capital) (x_1) in all countries; r = 0.34, p = 0.00, N = 152.

Structural Social Capital and Life Satisfaction

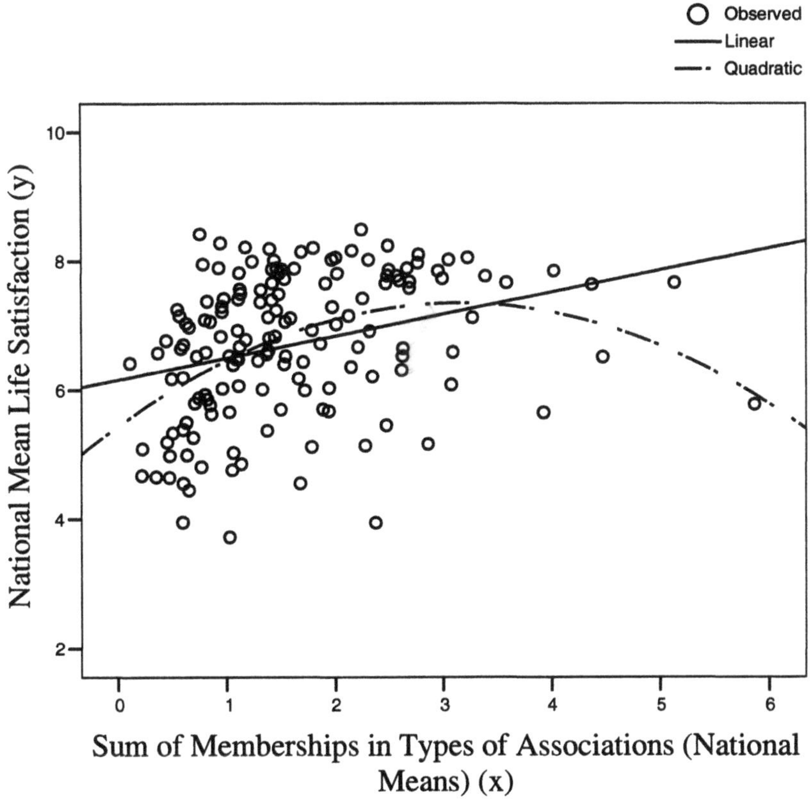

Figure 10: National mean life satisfaction (y) and average number of memberships in types of associations (structural social capital) (x_2) in all countries; $r = 0.31$, $p = 0.00$, $N = 152$.

Assuming a linear relationship between structural social capital and national mean life satisfaction, the correlation here is significant ($p = 0.00$), positive and moderate with $r = 0.31$. This result supports hypothesis 2. The regression equation for a linear model in this case is $y = 6.2 + 0.34 \cdot x$, meaning that for every point increase on the membership scale, the life satisfaction score would rise by 0.34 points, starting from an intercept of 6.2 if the average number of memberships in a society was 0.

However, there are reasons to assume the correlation between structural social capital and life satisfaction to be curvilinear in the shape of an inverted U for the 152 countries studied here: The quality of the curvilinear model is indicated by the higher R square for the quadratic model (R square = 0.17), compared to a lower R square = 0.09 of the linear model. To be completely sure of the nature of the correlation between the two variables, a quadratic variable of structural social capital (sum of memberships · sum of memberships) will later be included in the regression analysis, too. But indeed already the bivariate analysis indicates that membership in only a moderate number of types of associations per person enhances national average life satisfaction, in accordance with Putnam's findings (2000: 332, see figure 7). While the curvilinear curve rises at first, too much civic engagement above the carrying capacity of membership in 3.0 types of associations lowers life satisfaction, possibly due to stress. The equation for the curvilinear model is $y = 5.4 + 1.2 \cdot x - 0.2 \cdot x^2$. In other words, if the average membership score is 0, the national mean life satisfaction would be 5.4. For every point increase on the average membership scale, the life satisfaction score of a country rises in total, unless scores of the membership variable have become high enough to let the squared negative effect ($-0.2 \cdot x^2$) be more prominent and life satisfaction scores fall again[51].

[51] Excluding the outlier with an average membership rate of 5.78 did not bring about a significant change to the quality of the quadratic model.

The assumption that stress is responsible for the falling curve above three memberships is further supported when looking at active and inactive membership and their respective association with life satisfaction separately. It is mainly active membership that creates the curvilinear effect: The variable of the more demanding active membership shows a curve that falls steeper than the curve of inactive membership. In addition, the carrying capacity of the latter is higher (2.4) than that of the former (1.3).

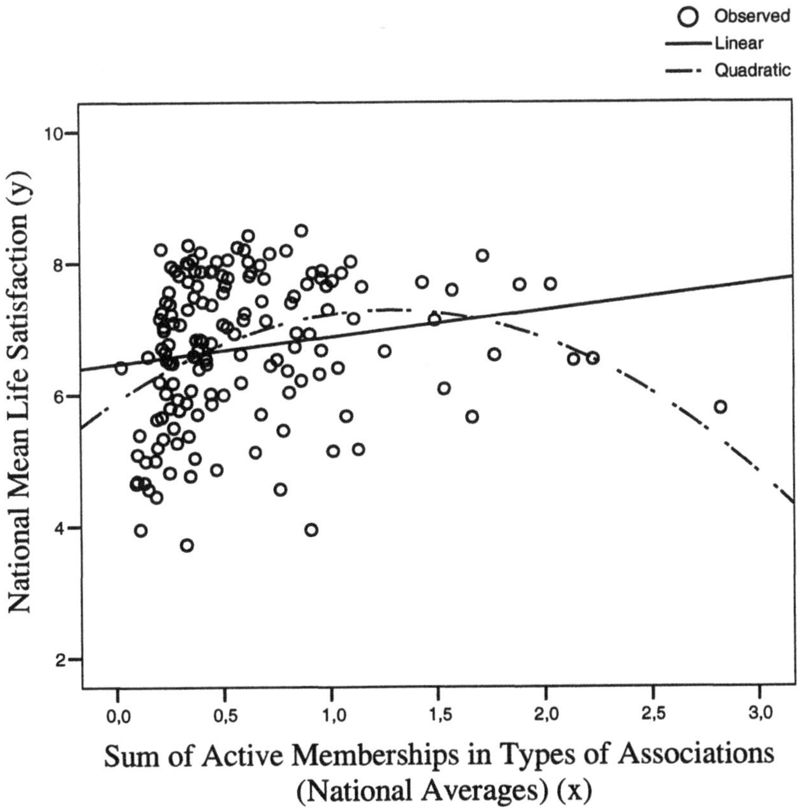

Figure 11: National mean life satisfaction (y) and average a*ctive* memberships in types of associations (x_{2a}) in all countries; $r = 0.17$, $p = 0.03$, $N = 152$.

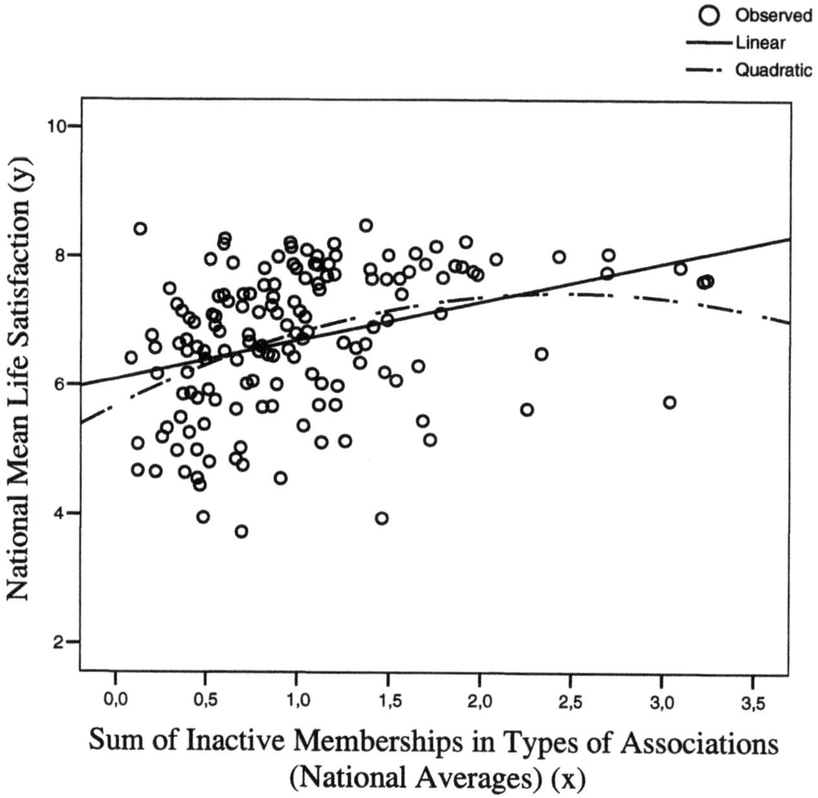

Figure 12: National mean life satisfaction (y) and average *inactive* memberships in types of associations (x_{2b}) in all countries; $r = 0.35$, $p = 0.00$, $N = 152$.

That is to say that above a certain threshold, active membership lowers life satisfaction faster and more intensely than inactive membership (presumably due to the more demanding nature of active engagement), and that this threshold is lower for active membership. People's life satisfaction therefore seems to suffer less from a high number of inactive memberships than from a high number of active memberships, as the curve estimations in figures 11 and 12 indicate.

The association between active memberships and life satisfaction as shown in figure 11 seems to be curvilinear with the R square = 0.11, as opposed to a lower R square = 0.03 in the linear model. The regression equation of the quadratic model as illustrated above is $y = 5.9 + 2.2 \cdot x - 0.84 \cdot x^2$. For a linear model, the regression equation is $y = 6.5 + 0.41 \cdot x$ and the association is weak, positive and significant ($p = 0.03$) with $r = 0.17$.

As briefly described earlier, the curvilinear curve of inactive membership in figure 12 falls less steep than that of active participation, and the carrying capacity is higher in the case of inactive membership. Also, the differences between the R square of a linear model (0.12) and of a quadratic model (0.15) are smaller, further indicating that the decrease of life satisfaction above the carrying capacity for inactive memberships is small. Finally, the shape of the curvilinear curve comes closer to a linear, positive graph than in the case of active membership. For the quadratic model, the equation is $y = 5.7 + 1.4 \cdot x - 0.29 \cdot x^2$. For the linear curve, the equation is $y = 6.1 + 0.6 \cdot x$ and the association is moderate, positive and highly significant ($p = 0.00$) with $r = 0.35$.

To conclude, the curvilinear curve fits best to describe the relationship between structural social capital and life satisfaction, as also indicated by the higher R square of the quadratic model compared to the linear one. Strictly speaking, this would mean that hypothesis 2 cannot be supported. Nevertheless, a positive relationship applies to most countries since 91.5 per cent of all cases are located below the carrying capacity of membership in 3 types of associations. Below 3 types of associations, the negative effect of too many memberships has not become prominent yet; the relationship is still positive here. In consequence, the hypothesis will be considered to be supported by the bivariate analysis. Similarly, the association between structural social capital and life satisfaction will be treated as linear when interpreting the beta coefficients in the forthcoming multivariate regression analysis. This will also be done in order to closely parallel previous literature. However, to be sure about the nature of the association between structural social capital and life satisfaction, the regression analysis will contain one model with both a linear and a quadratic variable of structural social capital.

Linking Social Capital and Life Satisfaction

Contrary to the theoretical assumption, the association between linking social capital and life satisfaction is extremely weak and non-significant ($p = 0.45$), although the coefficient is at least slightly positive with $r = 0.06$. However, it seems more appropriate to speak of a non-association here, as the R square of 0.004 further reinforces. The regression equation is $y = 6.0 + 0.27 \cdot x$.

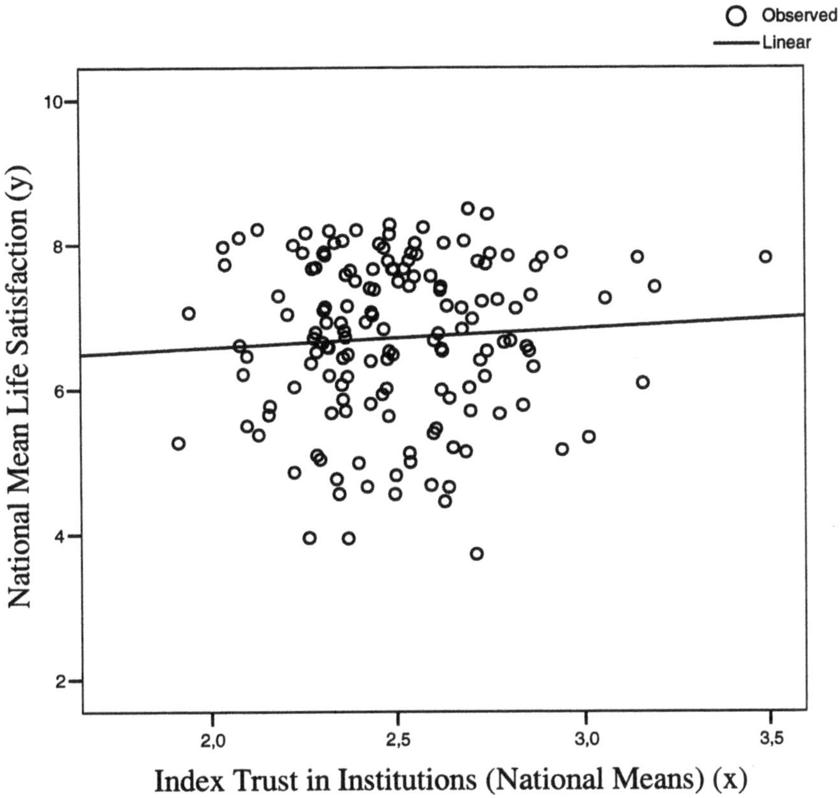

Figure 13: National mean life satisfaction (y) and national mean index trust in institutions (linking social capital) (x_3) in all countries; $r = 0.06$, $p = 0.45$, $N = 152$.

7.1.2 Multivariate Regression Analysis

The bivariate analyses have shown positive, significant and moderate relationships between at least the cognitive and structural social capital variables and life satisfaction, as hypothesised earlier. However, in order to test if the associations are robust, a multivariate regression analysis needs to be conducted. To assess the exact isolated effects of social capital on national mean life satisfaction, other covariates that might have an effect on the dependent variable will be controlled in the regression.

Table 8 contains standardised beta coefficients to compare the importance of the effect of each respective variable on national mean life satisfaction (y). The first model displays the control variables. Due to the relatively small size of the sample, this study focuses on important control variables for life satisfaction only. Hence, the control variables represent absolute (GDP per capita) and relative (Gini coefficient) economic possibilities, as well as economic uncertainty (inflation and unemployment rate).

GDP enters with a very large, positive and significant coefficient while unemployment has a significant, moderate, negative effect on life satisfaction. As predicted, these results indicate that the higher a country's GDP per capita and the lower its unemployment rate, the higher the nation's life satisfaction score will be. The other two standardised coefficients in model 1 are not significant[52].

---

[52] The effect of inflation is extremely weak although it still goes into the predicted negative direction. The Gini coefficient displays a weak but positive association with the dependent variable, pointing towards a high life satisfaction in countries with low income equality, which is contrary to the hypothesis. However, such a seemingly confusing effect has been observed before (Bjørnskov 2003, Donovan et al. 2002, Mulgan 2004) and could be due to a higher perceived social mobility among citizens if income equality is low. According to this logic, a higher Gini coefficient signals greater rewards for moving up in society. Another interpretation could be that people do not perceive the rich in their society as a reference group for social comparisons anymore if income differences are too large.

Table 8: Multivariate Regression Analysis for all Countries

	1	2	3	4	5	6
Constant	5.867*** (15.654)	5.596*** (14.262)	5.771*** (15.370)	5.414*** (7.112)	4.689*** (5.671)	5.210*** (12.833)
GDP per capita	0.547*** (6.940)	0.494*** (6.025)	0.499*** (6.018)	0.538*** (6.711)	0.510*** (6.091)	0.488*** (6.097)
Gini coefficient	0.100 (1.335)	0.070 (0.921)	0.073 (0.957)	0.088 (1.146)	0.074 (0.960)	0.075 (1.021)
Inflation rate	-0.032 (-0.434)	-0.010 (-0.141)	-0.015 (-0.199)	-0.041 (-0.543)	-0.008 (-0.11)	-0.004 (-0.053)
Unemployment rate	-0.210** (-2.827)	-0.202** (-2.758)	-0.201** (-2.731)	-0.215** (-2.872)	-0.215** (-2.926)	-0.217** (-3.035)
Cognitive social capital (gener. trust)		0.159* (-2.061)			0.913+ (1.885)	
Structural soc. cap. (sum memberships)			0.137+ (1.758)		-0.772 (-1.583)	0.802*** (3.505)
Linking soc. cap. (trust in institutions)				0.051 (0.684)	0.018 (0.238)	
Structural soc. cap. *quadratic* (SSC · SSC)						-0.695** (-3.078)
Observations	125	125	125	125	125	125
Durbin-Watson-Coefficient	1.58	1.53	1.52	1.58	1.50	1.51
R square	0.383	0.399	0.404	0.385	0.418	0.443
Adjusted R square	0.362	0.379	0.373	0.360	0.383	0.415

All coefficients except constants are standardised (OLS estimates); t-statistics in parentheses; *** indicates significance at $p \leq 0.001$, ** $p \leq 0.01$, * $p \leq 0.05$ and + $p \leq 0.1$.

When cognitive social capital is included in model 2, the effects of GDP and unemployment are slightly reduced and cognitive social capital shows a positive, weak and significant effect on life satisfaction, thereby supporting hypothesis 1. The same is true for structural social capital (model 3) and hypothesis 2, although the coefficient is a little weaker and only significant when choosing a confidence interval of 10 per cent. Finally, just like during the bivariate analysis, there is basically no effect from linking social capital on life satisfaction, even though the coefficient is positive, as hypothesised (model 4). Model 5, in which all types of social capital are included, shows distorted scores for the coefficients due to multicollinearity (i.e. the correlation between two independent variables is above $r = 0.60$ in accordance with Brosius 2006; here: between structural and cognitive social capital). It follows that model 5 cannot be used in the interpretation.

Finally, Model 6 serves to determine the exact nature of the correlation between structural social capital and life satisfaction. For this purpose, structural social capital (SSC) and its quadratic variable (SSC · SSC) are included. In line with the assumptions made during the bivariate analyses, the association is indeed curvilinear. That is to say that memberships in a few (up to 3, see figure 10) types of organisations per person are positively associated with life satisfaction levels, while too many memberships lead to decreased SWB-levels. This result can be seen by the fact that the coefficients in model 6 for both structural social capital and its quadratic variable are significant, while the former is positive but the latter is negative. The association between structural social capital and life satisfaction is curvilinear in the shape of an inverted U. However, the bivariate scatterplots had shown that most countries are below the carrying capacity of 3 types of organisations. Consequently, a positive association between structural social capital and life satisfaction applies to most nations.

The Durbin Watson coefficient as a test for autocorrelation, which should ideally be between 1.5 and 2.5 (Brosius 2006), indicates acceptable scores for all models. Furthermore, the tolerance scores of the variables in the study have all been checked to be within the acceptable range close to 1.0.

In conclusion, the positive, significant and moderate correlation that could be revealed during the bivariate analyses for cognitive social capital remains significant and can largely be confirmed despite the presence of important control variables such as GDP and unemployment rate. The positive effect of structural social capital on life satisfaction remains significant only at a confidence level of 10 per cent. The importance of the effect of social capital seems to be lowered in the presence of the economic control variables, though, as indicated by the relatively low beta values of cognitive and structural social capital (for further discussion see chapter 8.1). All in all, GDP has the biggest effect on the dependent variable, as its large beta coefficient suggests, followed by the unemployment rate and cognitive social capital.

Overall, the explanatory power of all models is quite high. Model 2 has the most explanatory power with an adjusted R square = 0.379, meaning that about 38 per cent of the variance can be explained by the independent variables in this model. The regression equation of this powerful model, when not listing insignificant control variables, is as follows:

$$y = 5.596 + 0.063 \cdot \text{GDP per capita (in 1000 US-\$)} - 0.037 \cdot \text{unemployment rate (in per cent)} + 0.013 \cdot \text{generalised trust (in per cent)}$$

Size of the Effect

On the basis of this regression equation, the size of the effect of social capital can be calculated. Speaking in statistical terms and all other factors being equal, if the percentage of people in a country who say that "most people can be trusted" increased by 20 per cent, the national mean life satisfaction would rise by 0.26 points on the 10 point scale. Such an increase in life satisfaction could equally be reached if the GDP per capita of a country grew by 4,126 US-$ or the unemployment rate was lowered by 7 percentage points. Consequently, increasing cognitive social capital would be as rewarding for the life satisfaction level of a society as creating a fairly high additional amount of material wealth, or as lowering the unemployment rate by a sizeable percentage (considering, for example, a total unemployment rate of 8.4 in Germany [1999] in the dataset).

The regression equation including *structural* social capital is (based on model 6):

$$y = 5.210 + 0.062 \cdot \text{GDP per capita (in 1000 US-\$)} - 0.040 \cdot \text{unemployment rate (in per cent)} + 0.903 \cdot \text{sum memberships in types of associations} - 0.175 \cdot \text{sum memberships in types of associations}^2$$

The equation suggests that if the number of average memberships per person in a country in this sample increased from 1 to 3 types of associations, the national mean life satisfaction would rise by 0.41 points on the 10 point scale[53]. This effect is equal to a rise in GDP

[53] Of course, this is statistical language with regard to the findings in the sample and the life satisfaction level would not *literally* rise immediately in practice when people in a country have signed up for more associations. Rather, the mechanisms by which social capital enhances SWB, as described in chapter 2.4, would be responsible for a long-term increase of life satisfaction. For a larger number of

per capita of 6,613 US-$ or a decrease in the unemployment rate by 10 percentage points. Again, the economic compensation that is necessary to match the enhancing effect of a rise in social capital on life satisfaction is quite high. Considering a mean unemployment rate of 9.28 per cent and a mean GDP per capita of 12,141 US-$ in the sample, the economic figures that can bring about the same rise of national mean life satisfaction as the increase in structural social capital represent a plus of 54 per cent of the mean GDP and a decrease in the unemployment rate of (theoretically) 108 per cent of the mean scores in the sample.

7.2 Rich Countries: Effect of Social Capital Even More Important than Effect of Income

According to the theoretical remarks and previous studies, one can assume the effects of social capital to be even more visible in richer nations. The economic approach in particular has revealed that the importance of GDP diminishes above a certain threshold of approximately 13,000 US-$ GDP per capita/year (see chapter 2.2). In order to take a closer look at the effect of social capital on life satisfaction vis-à-vis economic factors, a further analysis shall finally be run for rich countries, as well as poor and middle-income countries separately.

With respect to the findings of Inglehart/Klingemann (2000), countries with a GDP per capita above 13,000 US-$ will be classified as rich (49 observations in this sample), countries below that threshold will be considered poor and middle-income (97

---

memberships the effect would decrease due to the curvilinear nature of the association.

observations)[54]. This analysis will for the most part exclude linking social capital, since no effect of it on life satisfaction could be found in the previous chapters. Furthermore, models with multicollinearity will not be displayed either. As explained earlier, the fact that most countries have an average membership rate below the carrying capacity allows for the quadratic structural social capital variable to be left out of the regression analysis and to treat the relationship between structural social capital and SWB in part as linear.

7.2.1 Bivariate Analysis

It can be seen in figures 14 and 15 that the association for both cognitive and structural social capital with life satisfaction is positive, fairly strong and highly significant in rich countries. For these 49 cases, the correlation coefficient is $r = 0.49$ (structural social capital) and $r = 0.54$ (cognitive social capital) with $p = 0.00$. That is to say that, if we look at the rich countries exclusively, the effect of social capital on life satisfaction is much more remarkable than when investigating all 152 cases of the cross-country sample.

---

[54] Similar to the previous regression analysis, due to missing values for some control variables, the number of cases will be reduced to 44 and 81 respectively once control variables enter the multivariate analysis.

Cognitive Social Capital and Life Satisfaction in Rich Countries

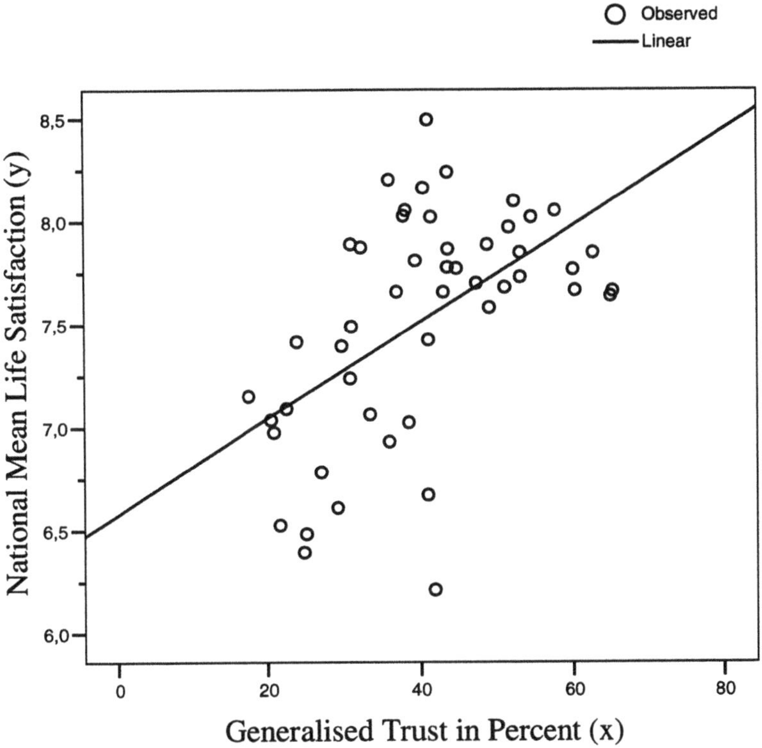

Figure 14: National mean life satisfaction (y) and generalised trust (cognitive social capital) (x_1) in rich countries; r = 0.54; p = 0.00; N = 49.

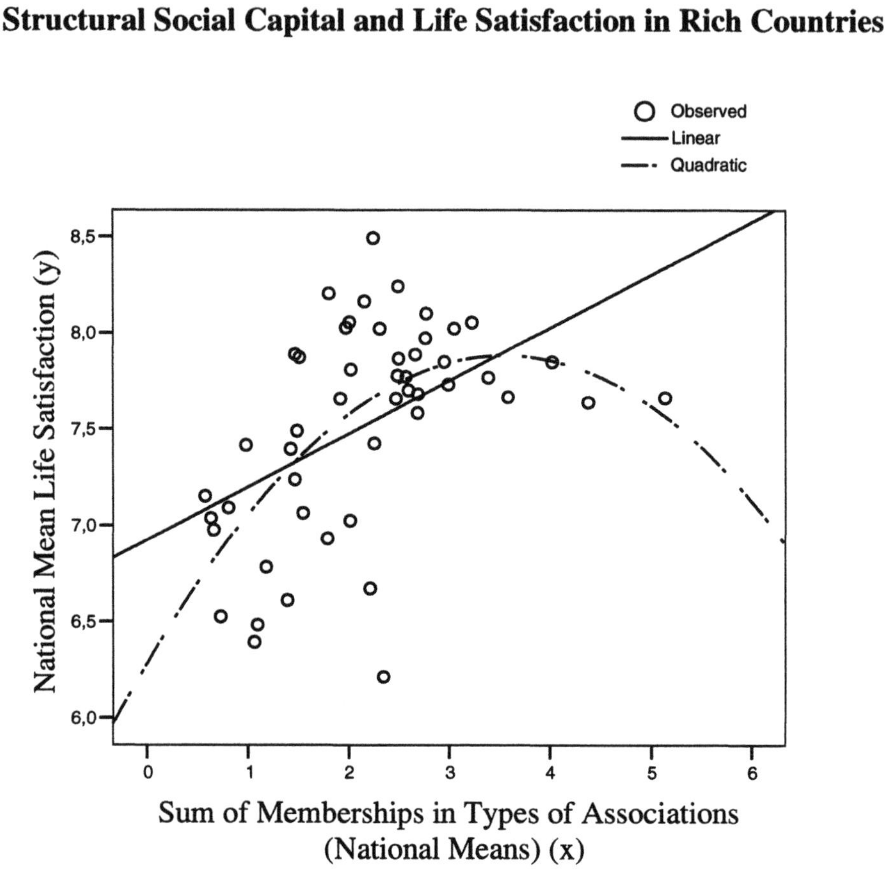

Figure 15: National mean life satisfaction (y) and average memberships in types of associations (structural social capital) (x2) in rich countries; $r = 0.49$, $p = 0.00$, $N = 49$.

7.2.2 Multivariate Regression Analysis

Similar to the preceding regression analysis, GDP has the biggest effect on life satisfaction among the control variables in model 1 of table 9, whereby no other control variable is significant this time. Furthermore, the coefficient of GDP is considerably smaller in this analysis compared to the previous one. Moreover, the coefficient even loses significance and sizeable importance once cognitive social capital is introduced. In fact, the strong, positive and significant effects of both cognitive (model 2) and structural (model 3) social capital exceed the importance of GDP for life satisfaction in the rich countries. This remarkable finding confirms the assumption that income becomes less important for SWB when countries have reached a certain level of living. All in all, first cognitive and then structural social capital exert the biggest effect on life satisfaction of all variables. Only linking social capital does not show an effect on the dependent variable again, although the positive coefficient is higher than in the first regression analysis.

Model 2 has most explanatory power, whereas its adjusted R square is lower than in the foregoing analysis, which is probably in part due to the smaller sample size here. Nevertheless, 29 per cent of the variance can still be explained by this model. The Durbin-Watson coefficient is again within the 1.5 to 2.5 margin and tolerance scores were again deemed acceptable.

Table 9: Multivariate Regression Analysis for Rich Countries

	1	2	3	4
Constant	7.421*** (12.069)	6.787*** (11.374)	7.142*** (12.337)	7.011*** (8.349)
GDP per capita	0.394* (2.143)	0.282 (1.651)	0.277 (1.578)	0.330 (1.614)
Gini coefficient	-0.223 (-1.555)	-0.196 (-1.497)	-0.220 (-1.665)	-0.230 (-1.587)
Inflation rate	0.098 (0.562)	0.086 (0.544)	0.089 (0.547)	0.089 (0.501)
Unemployment rate	-0.152 (-0.984)	-0.068 (-0.472)	-0.086 (-0.591)	-0.166 (-1.057)
Cognitive social capital (generalised trust)		0.420** (3.035)		
Structural social capital (sum memberships)			0.386** (2.724)	
Linking social capital (index trust in institutions)				0.117 (0.723)
Observations	44	44	44	44
Durbin-Watson-Coefficient	2.33	2.44	2.47	2.38
R square	0.224	0.375	0.350	0.234
Adjusted R square	0.144	0.293	0.265	0.133

All coefficients except constants are standardised (OLS estimates); t-statistics in parentheses; *** indicates significance at $p \leq 0.001$, ** $p \leq 0.01$, * $p \leq 0.05$ and + $p \leq 0.1$.

Size of the Effect

The regression equation for cognitive social capital for the sample of the rich countries based on model 2 is as follows:

$$y = 6.787 + 0.023 \cdot \text{GDP per capita (in 1000 US-\$)} - 0.017 \cdot \text{Gini coefficient} + 0.016 \cdot \text{inflation (in per cent)} - 0.008 \cdot \text{unemployment rate (in per cent)} + 0.018 \cdot \text{generalised trust (in per cent)}$$

For a 20 per cent increase in a rich country of people who say that "most people can be trusted", the national mean life satisfaction would rise by 0.36 points. This effect corresponds to a rise in GDP per capita of 15,652 US-$ in this sample of rich countries. Consequently, the size of the effect of cognitive social capital is bigger here than in the overall sample including all countries and it takes more money in wealthy nations to match the effect of cognitive social capital. The high amount of necessary GDP increase to bring about a rise in life satisfaction is probably not only due to the importance of social capital, but also to the decreased relevance of material wealth for life satisfaction once basic needs are met (see threshold hypothesis, chapter 2.2).

The following equation applies with regard to structural social capital (based on an additional model including a quadratic variable of structural social capital).

$$y = 6.404 + 0.024 \cdot \text{GDP per capita (in 1000 US-\$)} - 0.012 \cdot \text{Gini coefficient} + 0.019 \cdot \text{inflation (in per cent)} - 0.008 \cdot \text{unemployment rate (in per cent)} + 0.660 \cdot \text{sum memberships in types of associations} - 0.092 \cdot \text{sum memberships in types of associations}^2$$

The equation suggests that if the citizens of a nation increased their number of memberships per person from 1 to 3 types of associations, the national mean life satisfaction would rise by 0.58 points. In comparison, such an outcome would require a rise in GDP per capita of noteworthy 24,167 US-$ in rich countries. This amount is equivalent to 110 per cent of the mean GDP per capita in the subsample.

7.3 Poor and Middle-Income Countries: Economic Factors (Still) More Prominent than Social Capital

7.3.1 Bivariate Analysis

In contrast to the richer nations, there is hardly any association between structural (r = 0.06), or cognitive social capital (r = 0.08) and life satisfaction for the poor and middle-income countries, as demonstrated in figures 16 and 17. The lack of correlations illustrates the lower importance of social capital (if measured by generalised trust and membership rates, see Limitations chapter 8.2 and Research Implications chapter 8.3) for poorer and middle-income countries, as opposed to the stronger impact of social capital in richer countries presented in the previous chapter.

Cognitive Social Capital and Life Satisfaction in Poor and Middle-Income Countries

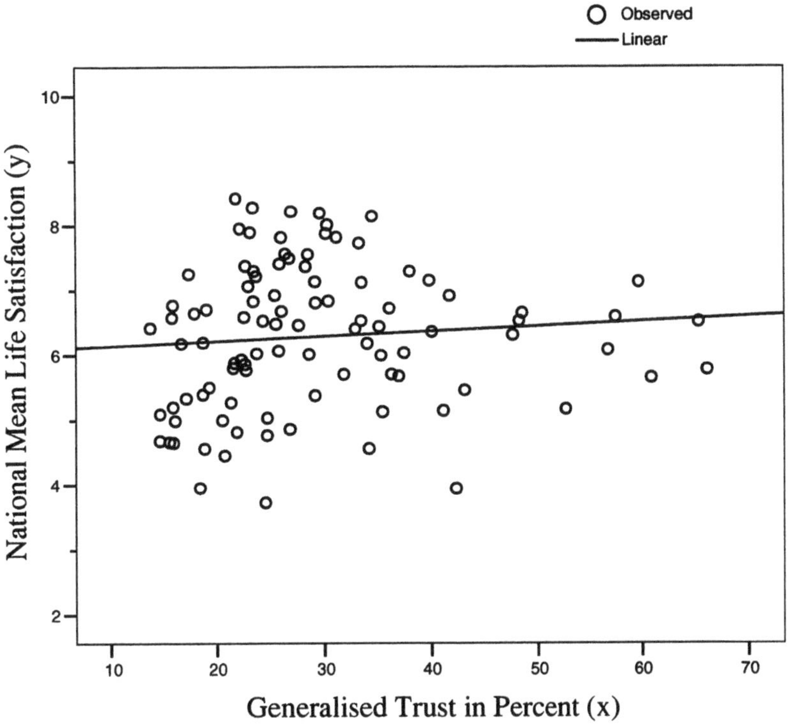

Figure 16: National mean life satisfaction (y) and generalised trust (cognitive social capital) (x1) in poor/middle-income countries; $r = 0.08$; $p = 0.42$; $N = 97$.

Structural Social Capital and Life Satisfaction in Poor and Middle-Income Countries

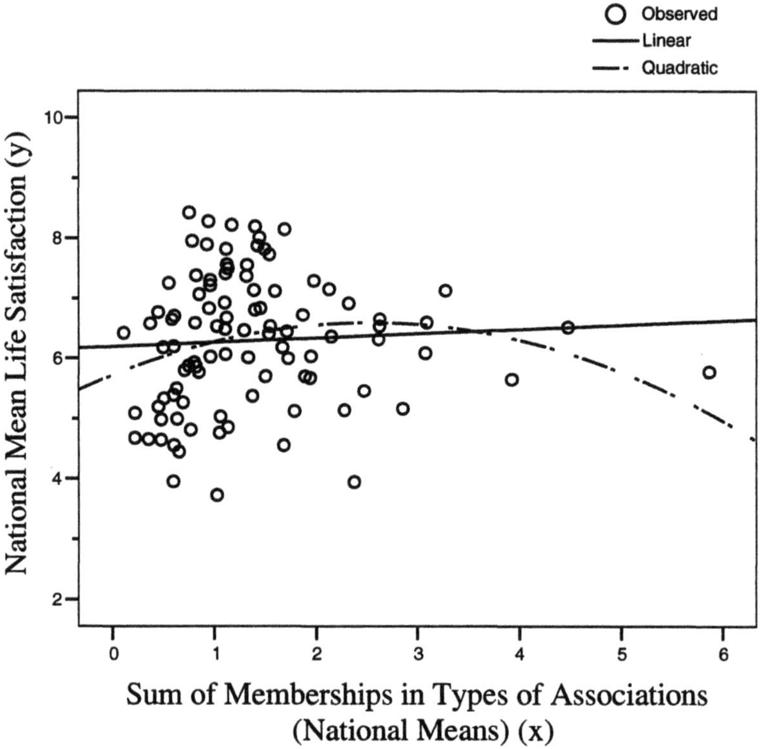

Figure 17: National mean life satisfaction (y) and average memberships in types of associations (structural social capital) (x_2) in poor and middle-income countries; $r = 0.06$; $p = 0.56$; $N = 97$.

7.3.2 Multivariate Regression Analysis

The economic control variables displayed in table 10 exert a remarkable effect on life satisfaction in poor and middle-income countries[55]. GDP, the Gini coefficient and the unemployment rate display significant beta coefficients, which are all in the predicted directions, again with the exception of the Gini coefficient. In particular, GDP has a very high, positive and significant coefficient, even in the presence of social capital variables. The effects of structural and cognitive social capital are moderate, positive and significant. However, they do not exceed the importance of the effect of GDP or the unemployment rate on life satisfaction in poor and middle-income countries. Model 2 is once more the one with most explanatory power and the highest adjusted R square, with more than 33 per cent being explained by its variables. The Durbin-Watson coefficient is moving towards critical levels of positive autocorrelation, especially in model 2 and 3, but the scores are still acceptable (Brosius 2006).

Size of the Effect

Finally, for the sample of the poor and middle-income countries, the regression equation for cognitive social capital based on model 2 is (including significant scores only):

$$y = 4.172 + 0.188 \cdot \text{GDP per capita (in 1000 US-\$)} - 0.053 \cdot \text{unemployment rate (in per cent)} + 0.026 \cdot \text{generalised trust (in per cent)}$$

[55] Compared to the overall sample of the first regression analysis, the variance in GDP between the countries in the sub-sample is not as high. Consequently, the large beta coefficients are very interesting because this sub-sample is fairly homogenous in terms of the countries' wealth, usually indicating that the coefficient of GDP should be relatively smaller (see also chapter 8.1).

Table 10: Multivariate Regression Analysis for Poor and Middle-Income Countries

	1	2	3	4
Constant	4.844*** (9.742)	4.172*** (7.723)	4.448*** (8.810)	3.375** (3.141)
GDP per capita	0.497*** (5.047)	0.567*** (5.771)	0.565*** (5.718)	0.511*** (5.212)
Gini coefficient	0.238* (2.426)	0.172+ (1.769)	0.177+ (1.813)	0.206* (2.078)
Inflation rate	-0.020 (-0.206)	0.031 (0.333)	0.028 (0.296)	-0.047 (-0.487)
Unemployment rate	-0.285** (-2.989)	-0.304*** (-3.304)	-0.296** (-3.221)	-0.304** (-3.185)
Cognitive social capital (generalised trust)		0.270** (2.678)		
Structural social capital (sum memberships)			0.257* (2.544)	
Linking social capital (index trust in institutions)				0.154 (1.539)
Observations	81	81	81	81
Durbin-Watson-Coefficient	1.55	1.46	1.49	1.55
R square	0.312	0.372	0.367	0.333
Adjusted R square	0.276	0.331	0.325	0.289

All coefficients except constants are standardised (OLS estimates); t-statistics in parentheses; *** indicates significance at $p \leq 0.001$, ** $p \leq 0.01$, * $p \leq 0.05$ and + $p \leq 0.1$.

The equation suggests that if the percentage of people who claim that "most people can be trusted" went up by 20 per cent in a poor or middle-income country, the national mean life satisfaction would rise by 0.52 points. Consequently, the potential increase of life satisfaction would be higher here than for the rich nations. This could be due to the lower average life satisfaction of the poor and middle-income countries (6.29) compared to the richer nations (7.52), which means that the potential for improvements is larger in poorer societies. More importantly, though, it would take an increase in GDP per capita by only 2,766 US-$ to create an equal rise in life satisfaction here - a lower sum compared to the rich nations and the total sample. This lower amount points towards the high importance of GDP and the sizeable effect that a rising national income can have for life satisfaction in poor and middle-income countries. Nonetheless, social capital is worth enhancing, since the amount mentioned above still is equivalent to 41 per cent of the mean GDP per capita in the sub-sample.

Finally, the equation for structural social capital is (based on an additional model with a quadratic structural social capital variable)

$$y = 4.058 + 0.176 \cdot \text{GDP per capita (in 1000 US-\$)} - 0.016 \cdot \text{Gini coefficient} + 0.055 \cdot \text{unemployment rate (in per cent)} + 1.142 \cdot \text{sum memberships in types of associations} - 0.213 \cdot \text{sum memberships in types of associations}^2$$

If the people of a poor or middle-income country increased their number of memberships per person from 1 to 3 types of associations, the life satisfaction score of that country would rise by 0.58 points. This result could also be achieved if GDP per capita grew by 3,295 US-$, which corresponds to 49 per cent of the mean GDP per capita in the sub-sample. These scores further reinforce the explanations made in the preceding paragraph.

8. Conclusion

8.1 Central Outcome: A Positive and (Largely) Significant Effect whose Strength Varies between Rich and Poor Countries

Main Hypotheses (H1 – H3)

The aim of this study was to find an answer to the research question: "What are the effects of social capital on life satisfaction (at the cross-national level)?" For this purpose, a theoretical framework had been developed based on social capital theory. A cross-national empirical analysis then investigated the precise effects of prominent social capital variables on national mean life satisfaction. The analyses in chapter 7.1 have produced results for all countries in the sample: There is a positive, significant and moderate effect of cognitive and structural social capital on life satisfaction for the nations examined in this investigation. Moreover, this relationship emerges as robust to testing for a set of control variables in the multivariate regression analysis[56]. Although, it has to be mentioned that the social capital coefficients lost strength in the presence of economic variables, compared to the moderate coefficients during the bivariate analyses. Meanwhile, there is no observable effect of linking social capital on life satisfaction. Hypotheses 1 and 2 can therefore be confirmed, while hypothesis 3 cannot. The results for the countries examined here support the notion that the more cognitive and structural social capital there is in a society, the higher is the nation's mean life satisfaction score.

[56] The effect was significant for structural social capital in the presence of control variables only at a confidence level of 10 per cent, though.

Interestingly though, the association between structural social capital and life satisfaction was revealed to be curvilinear. Membership in only a moderate number of types of associations per person enhances national average life satisfaction, which strictly speaking contradicts hypothesis 2. However, 91.5 per cent of all cases in this sample are located below the carrying capacity of average membership in 3 types of associations. Consequently, a positive relationship still applies to the overwhelming majority of countries and hypothesis 2 can under these circumstances largely be considered confirmed.

Rich vs. Poor and Middle-Income Countries (H4 – H7)

The observed decrease or even lack of an effect of economic factors on SWB in rich countries from previous studies (Easterlin 1974, Inglehart/Klingemann 2000) served as an encouragement to conduct additional analyses for rich and poor countries separately. An investigation in chapter 7.2 showed the effect of cognitive and structural social capital on life satisfaction to be even more important and significant for rich countries. Indeed, in those wealthy nations, the importance of the effect of social capital exceeds that of any other factor in the study, notably economic variables such as GDP and the unemployment rate. In contrast, the effects of the latter two variables are stronger than those of social capital in poor and middle-income countries (see chapter 7.3). The same is true for the overall sample of 125 cases. Nonetheless, cognitive and structural social capital did exert a moderate, positive effect on life satisfaction even in poorer countries.

With regard to the theoretical background, it can be concluded that the social capital approach as a way to explain differences in life satisfaction levels can all in all successfully be applied to the sample, particularly to the rich nations. The mechanisms by which social capital enhances life satisfaction seem to contain reasonable explanatory power. Only linking social capital did not show an effect on life satisfaction. In this particular case, Easterlin's (2000) assumption might indeed be true, that political influences from the public sphere do not to influence individuals' well-being. At least, the alleged powerlessness and helplessness that a lack of linking social capital was believed to bring about did not translate into a decreased life satisfaction.

The results also demonstrate that the economic approach to explaining differences in national SWB-levels is a powerful theory, especially in poor and middle-income countries. GDP and the unemployment rate were found to have the biggest effect on life satisfaction there. However, economic factors lose their explanatory power in countries above the level of 13,000 US-$ GDP per capita/year. The results thus support the "threshold hypothesis" (chapter 2.2) to some extent. In rich nations, the effect of social capital is more important than that of any economic factor in this study: social capital literally "trumps" money there. The social capital approach therefore gains explanatory power, the higher a country moves up on the development scale. Subsequently, improving GDP seems to be the primary approach when trying to enhance the SWB in poor and middle-income countries, while improving social capital seems more feasible in rich nations, where basic needs are already met.

The distinction between rich and poor countries is further illustrated by the size of the effect of social capital versus GDP on life satisfaction. The statistical results allow for the following calculations: For example, an increase of membership from 1 to 3 types of associations per person in a *poor* country would lead to the same improvement in national mean life satisfaction as would a rise in GDP per capita of approximately 3,300 US-$ (49 per cent of the mean GDP per capita in the poor nations' sample). Interestingly, in wealthy nations the same increase in average memberships would produce a rising mean life satisfaction that would take about *24,200 US-$* to match (*110 per cent* of the mean GDP per capita in the rich nations' sample). This discrepancy between rich and poor countries suggests two things: Further gains of wealth in rich countries would only be as rewarding for life satisfaction levels as improvements in social capital if the GDP increase was very large (in this example: more than doubling the GDP)[57]. At the same time, the beneficial effect of social capital for life satisfaction can more easily be matched by smaller increases in GDP in poor and middle-income countries. But the effect of social capital in poor nations is not to be underestimated – a combined development strategy featuring monetary and social capital seems appropriate.

Referring to table 3 above, the empirical results for a comparison of the importance of the effect of social capital vs. GDP in rich vs. poor nations correspond to the expectations expressed in chapter 3. That is to say that hypotheses 4 to 7 can be confirmed. Table 11 illustrates this finding. As predicted, the effects of social capital (here: for example cognitive social capital) on life satisfaction are more important in rich countries (β = 0.420**) than in poor ones (β = 0.270**) (confirming H4). Furthermore, the effects of GDP are more prominent in poor nations (β = 0.567***) than in rich ones (β = 0.282) (confirming H5). Likewise, the effect of social capital (β = 0.420**) is more important than the effect of GDP (β = 0.282) in rich nations (confirming H6), while the reverse is true in poor nations (β = 0.270** vs. β = 0.567***) (confirming H7).

[57] In this example it is assumed that the number of memberships would rise by 200 per cent (from 1 to 3 types of associations), which is of course a sizeable amount, too. However, tripling membership rates seems quite achievable compared to doubling the GDP per capita of an industrialised country.

Table 11: The Observed and Hypothesised Relative Importance of the Effect of Cognitive Social Capital vs. GDP on Life Satisfaction in Rich vs. Poor Countries

Importance of the effect of...	rich countries	poor countries
...cognitive social capital	0.420** (++)	0.270** (+)
...GDP	0.282 (+)	0.567*** (++)

All coefficients are standardised (OLS estimates).
*** indicates significance at $p \leq 0.001$, ** = $p \leq 0.01$.
(++) = a relatively large beta value was expected; (+) = a relatively small beta value was expected

Last but not least, a comparison with the results for the overall sample shows that the importance of the effect of social capital is lower ($\beta = 0.159$*) in the total sample of 125 observations than in either rich or poor subgroup. This phenomenon is due to the fact that the subgroups are more homogenous in terms of their level of GDP than the overall sample. In the subgroups, this results in lower scores for the standardised GDP coefficient and higher scores of the social capital coefficient. In the overall sample though, the level of material wealth varies a lot more between the countries, leading to a high standardised GDP coefficient and lower social capital coefficients.

Control Variables (H8 – H11)

The findings for GDP and the unemployment rate support hypotheses 8 and 11. The higher the GDP per capita and the lower the unemployment rate in a country, the higher is the nation's mean life satisfaction score. The inflation rate did not show a correlation with the dependent variable, so its quality as an indicator for public uncertainty about the economy can be challenged. At least, the potential uncertainty did not bring about a diminished life satisfaction in this analysis. Finally, the positive (yet insignificant) effect of the Gini coefficient on life satisfaction is against the theoretical prediction, but indeed could be due to higher rewards for moving up in society, as discussed earlier. Consequently, the study offers no support for hypotheses 9 and 10.

8.2 Limitations

At this stage, limitations to this study need to be mentioned. Chapter 2.1.3 has given an overview of the methodological limitations of subjective measures of well-being. Of course, the criticism brought forward in general towards subjective indicators and international comparisons applies also to this study. Social capital and life satisfaction in the analysis are based on self-reports, making it subject to the problems discussed above. The breadth of these conclusions is therefore limited by the methodological weaknesses of the indicators and variables used.

Furthermore, five points of criticism shall be discussed here. First of all, the direction of causation between the dependent and independent variables is not unchallenged. Although a particular direction of causation (on the basis of the theoretical background) was chosen by defining the dependent and independent variables in the regression analysis, the possibility of reverse causation for social capital and life satisfaction does exist in theory. While two criterions of causality (association and lack of spuriousness) are largely fulfilled in this study, the temporal precedence criterion between social capital and life satisfaction may be disputed. On the one hand, it is possible for people to be happy as a result of the social capital surrounding them and the support they gain from it. But on the other hand, it is also plausible that people who are naturally happier tend to accumulate more social capital (von dem Knesebeck et al. 2005, Yip et al. 2006). Longitudinal, individual data would be helpful here. Moreover, people with more social capital are also likely to be more extroverted, which correlates positively with SWB and such outgoing personalities are more likely to be involved in community work anyways (Helliwell 2001)[58]. Nevertheless, studies that report an association between social capital (x) and suicide rates (y) underline the causal relationship from social capital to well-being (Argyle 1999, Helliwell 2006), since temporal precedence of social capital is definitely given there. All in all, this limitation will in this study be handled by referring to the theoretical framework outlining a causal relationship from social capital to life satisfaction, as developed above.

Second, there could be further variables that influence both social capital and life satisfaction (e.g. crime rate, poverty, bad governance) (Woolcock 1998). However, an extended causal model taking into account all possible third influences on (x) and (y) would exceed the frame of this book and such an investigation would ideally require a larger sample. The existence of other possible explanatory variables shall nonetheless be mentioned here.

Third, using national means always brings about a certain degree of generalisation. For each variable in every of the 156 countries (i.e. cases) used here, it would be ideal to also examine the deviation and skewness of every distribution and whether they are unipolar or bipolar. Nonetheless, the degree of generalisation is assumed to be of limited harm here, and since using the national means is common in the literature, they will be considered valid representations.

[58] These explanations apply primarily to the individual level. However, since the national mean scores are nothing but aggregated individual scores the limitations shall also be mentioned for this study.

Fourth, the measurement of membership does not yet take into account the varying intensities of social capital that more or less time consuming memberships in different organisations produce. Membership in some organisations requires more activity and creates more social capital than others, e.g. membership in a trade union vs. membership in a religious sect. As Fukuyama put it: "A bowling league is not, to say the least, capable of storming a beach" (Fukuyama 2000: 101; see also Freitag 2003). The measurement instrument would need to be improved to allow for assessment of the exact amount of social capital that certain memberships produce. Such an exact assessment was not possible with the data used in this study. Also, the WVS data on memberships only enquires about *types* of associations instead of the exact number of associations that the respondent is a member of.

Finally, cultural variations in the production of social capital may lead to measurement errors (von dem Knesebeck et al. 2005). For example, the notion to develop social networks through organisational membership may be an idea that is mainly limited to industrialised, Western nations. The concept of social capital as operationalised by Putnam could therefore possibly work for those countries only and not relate to the social capital in other societies, where it is rather produced through informal networks. In Latin America and China, for instance, social capital and network ties are strong within families but lower towards strangers (Fukuyama 2000). Consequently, overall cognitive social capital if measured by the generalised trust question would be very low, whereas trust towards an extensive family circle would be higher. This assumption could explain the lower average membership rate in poor and middle-income countries (1.37) compared to rich nations (2.11) in this study, as well as the lower trust rates (29.59 vs. 39.51 per cent) (see appendix). Unfortunately, a question concerning trust in family was missing in many countries, so that the variable could not be used in this analysis.

8.3 Research Implications

Cognitive and structural social capital did affect life satisfaction in the end. But why was the effect not more important? In particular, why did social capital not have a stronger influence in developing countries, considering its alleged capability to even overcome the hardship of an urban slum (Biswas-Diener/Diener 2001)? One reason for this phenomenon was the importance of the effect of economic factors. But moreover, a crucial point could be the measurement of social capital as it is used in mainstream research so far. The last aspect of the limitations shows that the indicators of structural and cognitive social capital are probably not very suitable for poor and middle-income countries. Instead, the measurement instrument of structural social capital has to be extended to informal networks outside of civic organisations. Especially in South American nations and Third World countries, membership rates are generally lower and networks are not necessarily institutionalised. Likewise, cognitive social capital as captured by generalised trust tends to be lower in poor countries, although we can assume the often larger family networks in many such countries to deliver a lot of trust in an extended family circle (Fukuyama 2000). A major challenge for future research on social capital must therefore be to develop and apply more refined measures of social capital to supplement the variables 'membership in associations' and 'generalised trust'. This would correct the methodological problems of social capital mentioned earlier, and thus paint a more realistic picture of the societal levels of social capital in many countries.

Another implication for future research results from the shortcomings of a large-scale national-level analysis. Simply speaking, there are also rich people in poor nations as well as vice versa. An additional individual level or multilevel analysis could take a closer look at the effects of social capital on life satisfaction in selected countries and produce results to complement the findings from this investigation.

8.4 Policy Implications

The results show that the effects of social capital are important and they can help to explain why people in some countries are more satisfied with their lives than people in others. Especially the variation between rich nations can be traced back to the influence of social capital. So what are the policy implications? For the OECD world, the findings (notably the effect of social capital exceeding that of GDP and unemployment in the regression analysis) suggest that encouraging citizens to get involved in civic associations up to a certain level and investing in measures to strengthen trust among people would probably lead to a more satisfied population. *How* to increase social capital and motivate people to get involved is going to be the next question, but the need for and the rewards of it could be pointed out clearly by the cross-national analysis. Further investments in economic growth seem to be less efficient than investments in social trust and civic life when trying to enhance national mean life satisfaction in countries above a threshold of 13,000 US-$ GDP per capita/year, in which most material needs are already met. Lane concludes in this respect that to increase their QOL, the Western advanced societies should move from an emphasis on money and economic growth to an emphasis on companionship (Lane 2000).

In this respect, public policy can neither order people to be happy, nor dictate how they should use their free time. But through the allocation of resources it can provide a framework that enables citizens to create healthy social environments. While people should not, and cannot, be forced to increase their civic engagements, public policy can at least remove the obstacles in order to improve the social capital in a society. The following ideas provide a starting point for public debate.

- People need to have the time and money to contribute their energy to civic organisations. Allowing them more time off work exclusively for their engagements would lower the threshold to 'get involved'. They and their employers should be compensated through tax benefits or direct payments for the civic engagement.
- It has proven essential to build up trust between citizens. Community initiatives and activities at the neighbourhood level aspire to create healthy environments. Those projects need to be strengthened and intensified.
- The incentives for citizens to participate in civic associations have to be extended. This can include enhanced public recognition through awards, as well as increasing the awareness of the beneficial effects of social capital for life satisfaction and societal well-being. The publication of this study aims to contribute to this endeavour.

For the poor and middle-income countries, the results indicate that enhancing GDP and lowering the unemployment rate would be the primary strategies to contribute to a more satisfied population. But also for these regions, the implications from this investigation for development strategy planning are not restricted to improving material wealth. The potential increase in public well-being from a rise in social capital was still remarkable, as the statistical example (49 per cent of the mean GDP per capita) in chapter 7.3.2 illustrated. If a satisfied population is the aim of policy-making then countries in transition have to preserve or build up strong horizontal ties. For when a nation progresses from poor to middle-income to rich, the relevance of GDP for life satisfaction levels diminishes while the importance of social capital grows, as the results have shown. Therefore, it would be wise to make sure that modernisation does not erupt the existing systems of support and trust between the citizens, but instead such networks would need to be strengthened and new ones to be created. It will be significant to focus on social capital next to economic prosperity in the future. Planning ahead and investing in social capital in economically advancing nations along the way would thus be sensible and rewarding policy strategies, as the results of this study emphasise.

Appendix

Descriptive Statistics of Rich vs. Poor and Middle-Income Countries

Rich Countries

Table 12: Descriptive Statistics of the Rich Countries only

variable	rich countries (n = 44)		
	mean of all nations	**standard deviation**	**range**
dependent variable:			
(y) life satisfaction, national means	7.45	0.53	6.21 – 8.24
independent variables:			
(x_1) cognitive social capital: generalised trust, national percentages	39.51	12.64	65.3 – 17.6
(x_2) structural social capital: membership, national means	2.11	1.01	0.57 – 5.13
(x2a) structural social capital: *active* membership, national means	0.72	0.43	0.23 – 2.03

variable	rich countries (n = 44)		
	mean of all nations	standard deviation	range
(x2b) structural social capital: *inactive* membership, national means	1.39	0.72	3.24 – 0.36
(x3) linking social capital: index trust in institutions, national means	2.49	0.27	1.94 – 3.49
control variables:			
GDP per capita, US-$	22,005	6,383	13,060 – 48,370
gini coefficient	31.48	6.12	21.90 – 48.10
inflation, per cent	3.32	2.88	-0.67 – 11.37
unemployment rate, per cent	7.34	4.25	2.10 – 22.70

Poor and Middle-Income Countries

Table 13: Descriptive Statistics of the Poor and Middle-Income Countries only

variable	poor and middle-income countries (n = 81)		
	mean of all nations	standard deviation	range
dependent variable:			
(y) life satisfaction, national means	6.31	1.11	3.73 – 8.42
independent variables:			
(x_1) cognitive social capital: generalised trust, national percentages	29.59	11.68	13.7 – 65.3
(x_2) structural social capital: membership, national means	1.37	0.85	0.11 – 4.47
(x2a) structural social capital: *active* membership, national means	0.58	0.46	0.03 – 2.23
(x2b) structural social capital: *inactive* membership, national means	0.79	0.46	0.08 – 2.33
(x3) linking social capital: index trust in institutions, national means	2.51	0.27	1.91 – 3.19

variable	poor and middle-income countries (n = 81)		
	mean of all nations	standard deviation	range
control variables:			
GDP per capita, US-$	6,782	3,355	779 – 12,720
gini coefficient	37.71	11.57	18.00 – 60.10
inflation, per cent	36.07	85.46	-1.17 – 555.38
unemployment rate, per cent	10.33	6.45	2.19 - 32.40

Comparing the descriptive statistics of the rich countries with that of the poor and middle-income countries in the sample, systematic differences can be identified. Not only is the average level of GDP per capita naturally lower in the latter group. It also features lower scores on all social capital variables, except linking social capital. Likewise, the inflation rate, unemployment rate and the Gini coefficient are higher in those poorer societies. Finally, the mean life satisfaction score is lower in poor and middle-income countries, too (1.14 points).

Descriptive Statistics of the 125 Cases (as Used in the Regression Analysis) only

Table 14: Descriptive Statistics of the Dependent and Independent Variables for the 125 Cases as Used in the Regression Analysis only

variable	**all countries (n = 125)**		
	mean of all nations	**standard deviation**	**range**
dependent variable:			
(y) life satisfaction, national means	6.71	1.09	3.73 – 8.42
independent variables:			
(x_1) cognitive social capital: generalised trust, national percentages	33.09	12.89	13.7 – 65.3
(x_2) structural social capital: membership, national means	1.63	0.97	0.11 – 5.13
(x2a) structural social capital: *active* membership, national means	0.63	0.45	0.03 – 2.23

variable	all countries (n = 125)		
	mean of all nations	standard deviation	range
(x2b) structural social capital: *inactive* membership, national means	1.0	0.63	0.08 – 3.24
(x3) linking social capital: index trust in institutions, national means	2.50	0.27	1.91 – 3.49

Comparing the descriptive statistics of the 125 cases that enter the regression analysis with the 152 cases that are used in the bivariate analyses (see chapter 6) it can be seen that both tables are almost identical. That is to say that the reduction of cases in the regression analysis to 125, due to missing values for certain control variables, probably produces the same results as would have a regression analysis with all 152 cases.

Freedom House Index and GDP per Capita

Civil liberties and political rights are captured by the Freedom House Index. This independent index assesses political freedom in societies on a one-to-seven scale, i.e. as an interval variable in the analysis. A mean index of both components (civil liberties and political rights) was created here and the scores were reverse coded to better reflect a positive relationship with the score seven representing the highest degree of freedom and one the lowest. The scores of the Freedom House Index are drawn from the website of the organisation[59].

Table 15: Descriptive Statistics of Freedom House Index

variable	mean of all nations	standard deviation	range
all countries (n = 125)			
Freedom House Index	5.68	1.56	1.0 – 7.0
rich countries (n = 44)			
Freedom House Index	6.72	0.58	3.5 – 7.0
poor and middle-income countries (n = 81)			
Freedom House Index	5.12	1.64	1.0 – 7.0

Table 16 shows that the bivariate correlation of the Freedom House Index with the control variable GDP is too high (r = 0.628**) to include both of them in the regression analysis, due to a risk of multicollinearity, according to the r = 0.6 limit described by Brosius (2006). As assumed during the theoretical remarks, an independent effect of political freedom on national life satisfaction levels

[59] Available from http://www.freedomhouse.org/template.cfm?page=5, accessed on 16 April 2007.

therefore cannot be proven in the presence of a GDP variable and the Freedom House Index did not enter the regression analysis.

Table 16: Bivariate Correlation of GDP and Freedom House Index ($r = 0.628$, $p = 0.01$)

N = 125	Freedom House Index
GDP per capita	r = 0.628**

** = Correlation is significant at the $p = 0.01$ level (2-tailed).

Mean Life Satisfaction Score for each Country and Survey Year

Table 17: Mean Life Satisfaction Score for each Country and Survey Year, N=152

Country [survey year]	Life satisfaction national means	Country [survey year]	Life satisfaction national means
Albania [1998]	4.77	Austria [1990]	7.87
Albania [2002]	5.17	Austria [1999]	8.03
Algeria [2002]	5.67	Azerbaijan [1997]	5.39
Argentina [1984]	6.77	Bangladesh [1996]	6.41
Argentina [1991]	7.25	Bangladesh [2002]	5.78
Argentina [1995]	6.93	Belarus [2000]	4.81
Argentina [1999]	7.30	Belgium [1981]	7.38
Australia [1981]	7.89	Belgium [1999]	7.43
Australia [1995]	7.58	Bosnia and Herzegovina [1998]	5.46

Bosnia and Hzgv. [2001]	5.77
Brazil [1991]	7.37
Brazil [1997]	7.15
Bulgaria [1990]	5.03
Bulgaria [1997]	4.66
Bulgaria [1999]	5.50
Canada [1982]	7.82
Canada [1990]	7.89
Canada [2000]	7.85
Chile [1990]	7.55
Chile [1996]	6.92
Chile [2000]	7.12
China [1990]	7.29
China [1995]	6.83
China [2001]	6.53
Colombia [1997]	8.19
Colombia [1998]	8.42
Croatia [1996]	6.18
Croatia [1999]	6.68
Czech Republic [1991]	6.83
Czech Republic [1998]	6.39
Czech Republic [1999]	7.06
Denmark [1981]	8.22
Denmark [1990]	8.16
Denmark [1999]	8.24
Dominican Republic [1996]	7.13
El Salvador [1999]	7.50
Estonia [1990]	6.00
Estonia [1996]	5.00
Estonia [1999]	5.93

Finland [1990]	7.68	Hungary [1999]	5.80
Finland [1996]	7.78	Iceland [1984]	8.06
Finland [2000]	7.87	Iceland [1990]	8.02
France [1981]	6.71	Iceland [1999]	8.05
France [1990]	6.78	India [1995]	6.53
Georgia [1996]	4.68	India [2001]	5.14
Germany West [1981]	7.22	Ireland [1981]	7.82
Germany [1990]	7.02	Ireland [1990]	7.88
Germany [1997]	6.93	Ireland [1999]	8.20
Germany [1999]	7.42	Italy [1981]	6.65
Great Britain [1981]	7.56	Japan [1981]	6.58
Great Britain [1990]	7.49	Japan [1990]	6.53
Great Britain [1999]	7.40	Japan [2000]	6.48
Greece [1999]	6.67	Korea (Republic of) [1982]	5.33
Hungary [1991]	6.03	Korea (Republic of) [2001]	6.21
Hungary [1998]	5.86	Kyrgyzstan [2003]	6.48

Latvia [1990]	5.70	Netherlands [1990]	7.77
Latvia [1999]	5.27	Netherlands [1999]	7.85
Lithuania [1990]	6.01	New Zealand [1998]	7.70
Lithuania [1997]	4.99	Nigeria [1995]	6.59
Lithuania [1999]	5.20	Northern Ireland [1981]	7.66
Luxembourg [1999]	7.81	Northern Ireland [1990]	7.88
Macedonia. Republic of [1998]	5.70	Northern Ireland [1999]	8.00
Macedonia. Republic of [2001]	5.12	Norway [1982]	7.89
Malta [1983]	7.95	Norway [1996]	7.66
Malta [1991]	8.28	Peru [1996]	6.36
Mexico [1990]	7.41	Peru [2001]	6.44
Mexico [2000]	8.14	Philippines [2001]	6.65
Moldova (Republic of) [1996]	3.73	Poland [1990]	6.53
Moldova (Republic of) [2002]	4.56	Poland [1997]	6.42
Netherlands [1981]	7.73	Poland [1999]	6.20

Portugal [1990]	7.07	Slovenia [1995]	6.46
Portugal [1999]	7.04	South Africa [1996]	6.08
Puerto Rico [1995]	8.10	South Africa [2001]	6.31
Puerto Rico [2001]	8.49	Spain [1981]	6.59
Romania [1993]	5.88	Spain [1990]	7.15
Romania [1998]	4.86	Spain [1995]	6.61
Russian Federation [1990]	5.37	Spain [1999]	7.09
Russian Federation [1995]	4.45	Spain [2000]	6.98
Russian Federation [1999]	4.65	Sweden [1982]	8.01
Serbia and Montenegro [1996]	5.66	Sweden [1990]	7.97
Serbia and Montenegro [2001]	5.63	Sweden [1996]	7.77
Singapore [2002]	7.24	Sweden [1999]	7.64
Slovakia [1991]	6.81	Switzerland [1996]	8.02
Slovakia [1998]	6.07	Taiwan Province of China [1994]	6.56
Slovakia [1999]	6.03	Turkey [1996]	6.18

Turkey [2001]	5.09	United States [1995]	7.67
Uganda [2001]	5.65	United States [1999]	7.66
Ukraine [1996]	3.95	Uruguay [1996]	7.13
Ukraine [1999]	4.56	Venezuela [1996]	6.72
United States [1982]	7.66	Viet Nam [2001]	6.52
United States [1990]	7.73	Zimbabwe [2001]	3.95

Source: EUROPEAN AND WORLD VALUES SURVEYS FOUR-WAVE INTEGRATED DATA FILE, 1981-2004, v.20060423, 2006. The European Values Study Foundation and World Values Survey Association. Aggregate File Producers: ASEP/JDS, Madrid, Spain/Tilburg University, Tilburg, the Netherlands. Aggregate File Distributors: ASEP/JDS and ZA, Cologne, Germany. Data file (.sav) available from www.worldvaluessurvey.org, accessed on 12 October 2006.

List of Figures and Tables

Figures

Tables

Bibliography

Adam, F. and Rončević, B., 2004. Social Capital as a Useful Scientific Metaphor. In: N. Genov, ed. *Advances in Sociological Theory*. Wiesbaden: Verlag fuer Sozialwissenschaften, 183-204.

Ahuvia, A., 2001. Traditional, Interpretive, and Reception Based Content Analysis to Address Issues of Pragmatic and Theoretical Concern. *Social Indicators Research*, 54, 139-172.

Allardt, E., 1993. Having, Loving, Being. An Alternative to the Swedish Model of Welfare Research. In: M. Nussbaum and A. Sen, eds. *The Quality of Life*. New York: Oxford University Press, 88-94.

Alesina, A., Di Tella, R. and MacCulloch, R., 2004. Inequality and Happiness: Are Europeans and Americans Different? *Journal of Public Economics*, 88, 2009-2042.

Alesina, A. and La Ferrara, E., 2000. *The Determinants of Trust*. NBER Working Paper 7621. Cambridge, MA: National Bureau of Economic Research.

Almond, G. and Verba, S., 1963. *The Civic Culture. Political Attitudes and Democracy in Five Nations*. Princeton: Princeton University Press.

Andrews, F.M. and Withey, S.B., 1976. *Social Indicators of Well-Being: Americans' Perceptions of Life Quality*. New York: Plenum Press.

Argyle, M., 1987. *The Psychology of Happiness*. London: Methuen.

Argyle, M., 1996. Subjective Well-Being. In: A. Offer, ed. *In Pursuit of the Quality of Life*. Oxford: Oxford University Press, 18-45.

Argyle, M., 1999. Causes and Correlates of Happiness. In: D. Kahnemann, E. Diener, N. Schwarz, eds. *Well-Being: The Foundations of Hedonic Psychology*. New York: Russell Sage Foundation, 353-373.

Aristotle, 1985. *Nicomachean Ethics. Translated by Terence Irwin*. Indianapolis: Hackett Publishing Company.

Balatsky, G., and Diener, E., 1993. Subjective Well-Being among Russian Students. *Social Indicators Research*, 28, 225-243.

Bargatzky, T., 2002. Contemplativus in Actione. Glücksvorstellungen im Kulturvergleich. In: A. Bellebaum, ed. *Glücksforschung: Eine Bestandsaufnahme*. Konstanz: UVK, 95-108.

Bellebaum, A., 2002. Glück: Erscheinungsvielfalt und Bedeutungsreichtum. In: A. Bellebaum, ed. *Glücksforschung: Eine Bestandsaufnahme*. Konstanz: UVK, 13-42.

Ben-Shlomo, Y., White, I.R. and Marmot, M., 1996. Does the Variation in the Socioeconomic Characteristics of an Area Affect Mortality. *British Medical Journal*, 312, 1013-1014.

Berger-Schmitt, R., 2000. *Dimensions, Indicators and Time Series in a European System of Social Indicators*. EuReporting Working Paper No. 16. Mannheim: Centre for Survey Research and Methodology (ZUMA).

Berger-Schmitt, R., 2002. Considering Social Cohesion in Quality of Life Assessment, Concept and Measurement. *Social Indicators Research*, 58, 403–428.

Berger-Schmitt, R. and Noll, H.-H., 2000. *Conceptual Framework and Structure of a European System of Social Indicators*. EuReporting Working Paper No. 9. Mannheim: Centre for Survey Research and Methodology (ZUMA).

Berkman, L. and Syme, L., 1979. Social Networks, Host Resistance and Mortality: A Nine-Year Follow-Up Study of Alameda County Residents. *American Journal of Epidemiology*, 109, 186–204.

Berkman, L.F., and Glass, T., 2000. Social Integration, Social Networks, Social Support, and Health. In: L.F. Berkman and I. Kawachi, eds. *Social Epidemiology*. Oxford: Oxford University Press, 137-173.

Bertand, M. and Mullainathan, S., 2001. *Do People Mean What They Say? Implications for Subjective Survey Data*. Cambridge, MA: MIT, Department of Economics, Working Paper Series.

Biswas-Diener, R., and Diener, E., 2001. Making the Best of a Bad Situation: Satisfaction in the Slums of Calcutta. *Social Indicators Research*, 55, 329–352.

Bjørnskov, C., 2003. The Happy Few: Cross-Country Evidence on Social Capital and Life Satisfaction. *Kyklos*, 56 (1), 3-16.

Black, J., 2003. *A Dictionary of Economics*. Oxford: Oxford University Press.

Blanchflower, D. G. and Oswald, A. J., 2000. *Well-Being over Time in Britain and the USA*. NBER Working Paper 7487. Cambridge, MA: National Bureau of Economic Research.

Blanchflower, D. G. and Oswald, A. J. 2005. Happiness and the Human Development Index: The Paradox of Australia. *Australian Economic Review*, 38, 307–318.

Bradburn. N., 1969. *The Structure of Psychological Well-Being*. Chicago: Aidine.

Bradburn, N.M. and Caplovitz, D., 1965. *Reports on Happiness. A Pilot Study of Behavior Related to Mental Health*. Chicago: Aldine.

Brehm, J. and Rahn, W., 1997. Individual-Level Evidence for the Causes and Consequences of Social Capital. *American Journal of Political Science*, 41(3), 999-1024.

Brickman, P., and Campbell, D. T., 1971. Hedonic Relativism and Planning the Good Society. In: M. H. Appley, ed. *Adaptation-Level Theory: A Symposium*. New York: Academic Press, 287-302.

Brosius, F., 2006. *SPSS 14*. Heidelberg: MITP.
Bourdieu, P., 1986. The Forms of Capital. In: J.G. Richardson, ed. *Handbook for Theory and Research for the Sociology of Education*. Westport, CT: Greenwood Press, 241-258.
Braun, H., 2002. Empirische Glücksforschung. Ein schwieriges Unterfangen. In: A. Bellebaum, ed. *Glücksforschung: Eine Bestandsaufnahme*. Konstanz: UVK, 43-58.
Brickman, P., Coates, D., and Janoff-Bulman, R., 1978. Lottery Winners and Accident Victims: Is Happiness Relative? *Journal of Personality and Social Psychology*, 36 (8), 917-927.
Bulmahn, T., 2000. Modernity and Happiness: The Case of Germany. *Journal of Happiness Studies*, 1, 375-400.
Calman, K.C., 1987. Definitions and Dimensions of Quality of Life. In: N.K. Aaronson and J. Beckmann, eds. *The Quality of Life of Cancer Patients*. New York: Raven, 1-9.
Camfield, L., 2004. Measuring SWB in Developing Countries. In: W. Glatzer, S. von Below, and M. Stoffregen, eds. *Challenges for the Quality of Life in Contemporary Societies*. Dordrecht: Kluwer, 45-60.
Campbell, A., 1972. Aspiration, Satisfaction and Fulfilment. In: A. Campbell and P. E. Converse, eds. *The Human Meaning of Social Change*. New York: Russell Sage Foundation, 441-446.
Campbell, A., Converse, P. E. and Rodgers, W. L., 1976. *The Quality of American Life: Perceptions, Evaluations, and Satisfactions*. New York: Russell Sage Foundation.
Cantril, H., 1967. *The Pattern of Human Concerns*. New Brunswick: Rutgers University Press.
Christoph, B. and Noll, H.-H., 2003. Subjective Well-Being in the European Union during the 1990's. *Social Indicators Research*, 64 (3), 521-546.

Clark, J., 1996. *Shifting Engagements: Lessons from the 'Bowling Alone' Debate*. Hudson Briefing Papers, no. 196. Indianapolis: Hudson Institute.

Clark, A. and Oswald, A., 1994: Unhappiness and Unemployment. *Economic Journal*, 104, 648-659.

Clark, A. and Oswald, A., 1996. Satisfaction and Comparison Income. *Journal of Public Economics*, 61 (3), 359-381.

Cobb, C. W., 2000. *Measurement Tools and the Quality of Life*. San Francisco: Redefining Progress.

Coleman, J. S., 1988. Social Capital in the Creation of Human Capital. *American Journal of Sociology*, 94, supplement, 95-120.

Coleman, J. C., 1990. *Foundations of Social Theory*. Cambridge, MA: Harvard University Press.

Costa, P.T., Zonderman, A.B., McCrae, R.R., Cornoni-Huntley, J., Lock, B.Z., and Barbano, H.E., 1987. Longitudinal Analyses of Psychological Well-Being in a National Sample: Stability of Mean Levels. *Journal of Gerontology*, 42, 50-55.

Cravens, D., Hills, G.E., 1978. Measurement Issues in Studying Marketing and Quality of Life. In: F.D. Reynolds and H.C. Barksdale, eds. *Marketing and the Quality of Life*. Chicago: American Marketing Association.

Creed, W.E.D. and Miles, R.E., 1996. Trust in Organisations: A Conceptual Framework Linking Organisational Forms, Managerial Philosophies and the Opportunity Costs of Controls. In: R.M. Kramer and T.R. Tyler, eds. *Trust in Organisations: Frontiers of Theory and Research*. Thousand Oaks, CA: Sage, 16-38.

Croson, R., 1999. *Other-Regarding Behavior in Economics*. CSWEP Newsletter, Winter. Tallahassee, FL: American Economic Association.

Crossley, A. and Langdridge, D., 2005. Understanding the Reasons for Happiness: A Network Analysis. *Journal of Happiness Studies*, 6 (2), 107-135.

Cummins, R.A., 1996. The Domains of Life Satisfaction: An Attempt to Order Chaos. *Social Indicators Research*, 38, 303-28.

Cummins, R.A., 2001. Living with Support in the Community: Predictors of Satisfaction with Life. *Mental Retardation and Developmental Disabilities Research Reviews*, 7, 99-104.

Cummins, R.A., Gullone, E., and Lau, A.L.D., 2002. A Model of Subjective Well-Being Homeostasis: The Role of Personality. In: E. Gullone and R.A. Cummins, eds. *The Universality of Subjective Well-Being Indicators*. Social Indicators Research Book Series, Volume 16. Dordrecht: Kluwer, 7-46.

Cutler, S. E., Bunce, S. C., and Larsen, R. J., 1996. Repressive Coping Style and its Relation to Daily Emotional Experience and Remembered Emotional Experience. *Journal of Personality*, 64, 379-405.

Csikszentmihalyi, M., 1997. *Finding Flow: The Psychology of Engagement with Everyday Life*. New York: Basic Books.

Daly, H.E. and Cobb, J.B., 1989. *For the Common Good. Redirecting the Economy toward Community. The Environment and a Sustainable Future*. Boston: Beacon Press.

Degele, N. and Dries, C., 2005. *Modernisierungstheorie. Eine Einführung*. München: Fink.

Delhey, J., 2004. *EU - Kluft zwischen West und Ost. Lebenszufriedenheit im erweiterten Europa*. Berlin: WZB-Mitteilungen.

Delhey, J., Böhnke, P., Habich, R. and Zapf, W., 2002. Quality of Life in a European Perspective. The Euromodule as a new Instrument for Comparative Welfare Research. *Social Indicators Research*, 58, 163-176.

Diener, E., 1984. Subjective Well-Being. *Psychological Bulletin*, 95, 542-575.

Diener, E., 2000. Subjective Well-Being: The science of Happiness and a Proposal for a National Index. *American Psychologist*, 55 (1), 34-43.

Diener, E., Diener, M., and Diener, C., 1995 (Diener et al. 1995a). Factors Predicting the Subjective Well-Being of Nations. *Journal of Personality and Social Psychology*, 69, 851-864.

Diener, E. and Emmons, R. A., 1985. The Independence of Positive and Negative Affect. *Journal of Personality and Social Psychology*, 47, 1105-1117.

Diener, E., Emmons, R.A., Larsen, R.J., and Griffin, S., 1985. The Satisfaction with Life Scale. *Journal of Personality Assessment*, 49, 71-75.

Diener, E., and Fujita, F., 1995. Resources, Personal Strivings, and Subjective Well-Being: A Nomothetic and Idiographic Approach. *Journal of Personality and Social Psychology*, 68, 926-935.

Diener, E. and Lucas, R.E., 1999. Personality and Subjective Well-Being. In: D. Kahnemann, E. Diener, N. Schwarz, eds. *Well-Being: The Foundations of Hedonic Psychology*. New York: Russell Sage Foundation, 213-229.

Diener, E. and Oishi, S., 2000. Money and Happiness: Income and Subjective Well-Being across Nations. In: E. Diener and E.M. Suh, eds. *Culture and Subjective Well-Being*. Cambridge, MA: Bradford, 185-218.

Diener, E. and Oishi, S., 2004. Are Scandinavians Happier than Asians? Issues in Comparing Nations on Subjective Well-Being. *Politics and Economics of Asia*, 10, 1-25.

Diener, E., Sandvik, E., Seidlitz, L., and Diener, M., 1993. The Relationship between Income and Subjective Well-Being: Relative or Absolute? *Social Indicators Research*, 28, 195-223.

Diener, E. and Suh, E.M., 1997. Measuring Quality of Life: Economic, Social, and Subjective Indicators. *Social Indicators Research*, 40, 189-216.

Diener, E. and Suh, E.M., 1999. National Differences in Subjective Well-Being. In: D. Kahnemann, E. Diener, N. Schwarz, eds. *Well-Being: The Foundations of Hedonic Psychology*. New York: Russell Sage Foundation, 434-451.

Diener, E. and Suh, E. M., 2000. Measuring Subjective Well-Being to Compare the Quality of Life of Cultures. In: E. Diener and E.M. Suh, eds. *Culture and Subjective Well-Being*. Cambridge, MA: Bradford, 3-12.

Diener, E., Suh, E. M., Lucas, R. E. and Smith, H. L., 1999. Subjective Well-Being: Three Decades of Progress. *Psychological Bulletin*, 125, 276–302.

Diener, E., Suh, E.M., Smith, H., and Shao, L., 1995 (Diener et al. 1995b). National Differences in Reported Subjective Well-Being: Why Do They Occur? *Social Indicators Research*, 34, 7-32.

Di Tella, R., MacCulloch, R. and Oswald, A., 2001. Preferences over Inflation and Unemployment: Evidence from Surveys of Happiness. *American Economic Review*, 91, 1, 335-341.

Diwan, R., 2000. Relational Wealth and the Quality of Life. *Journal of Socio-Economics*, 29, 4, 305-340.

Donovan, N., Halpern, D. and Sargeant, R., 2002. *Life Satsfaction: The State of Knowledge and Implications for Government*. London: Prime Minister's Strategy Unit.

Drenowski, J., 1974. *On Measuring and Planning the Quality of Life*. The Hague: Mouton.

Durkheim, E., 1893. *Über soziale Arbeitsteilung. Studie über die Organisation höherer Gesellschaften*. 2nd ed. Frankfurt am Main: Suhrkamp.

Easterlin, R.A., 1974. Does Economic Growth Improve the Human Lot? Some Empirical Evidence. In: P.A. David and M. Reder, eds.: *Nations and Households in Economic Growth.* New York: Academic Press, 89-125.

Easterlin, R. A., 1995. Will Raising the Incomes of All Increase the Happiness of All? *Journal of Economic Behavior and Organization*, 27, 35-48.

Easterlin, R. A., 2001. Life Cycle Welfare: Trends and Differences. *Journal of Happiness Studies*, 2, 1-12.

Easterlin, R. A., 2003. Income and Happiness: Towards a Unified Theory. *The Economic Journal*, 111, 465-84.

Easterlin, R.A., 2004. Life Satisfaction: Can We Produce It? In: W. Glatzer, S. von Below, and M. Stoffregen, ed. *Challenges for the Quality of Life in Contemporary Societies.* Dordrecht: Kluwer, 347-357.

Ebstein, R.P., Novick, O., Umansky, R., Priel, B., Osher, Y., Blaine, D., Bennett, E.R., Nemanov, L., Katz, M., Belmaker, R.H., 1996. Dopamine D4 Receptor (D4DR) Exon III Polymorphism Associated with the Human Personality Trait of Novelty Seeking. *Nature Genetics*, 12 (1), 78-80.

Emmons, R. A. and Diener, E., 1985. Personality Correlates of Subjective Well-Being. *Personality and Social Psychology Bulletin*, 11, 89-97.

Erikson, R., 1974. Welfare as a Planning Goal. *Acta Sociologica.* 17 (3), 273-288.

Erikson, R. and Aberg, R., 1987. The Nature and Distribution of Welfare. In: R. Erikson and R. Aberg, eds. *Welfare in Transition: A Survey of Living Conditions in Sweden 1968-1981.* Oxford: Clarendon, 1-14.

Erikson R. and Uusitalo, H., 1987. The Scandinavian Approach to Welfare Research. In: R. Erikson, ed. *The Scandinavian Model: Welfare States and Welfare Research.* New York: M.E. Sharpe, 177-193.

Erikson, R., 1993. Descriptions of Inequality: The Swedish Approach to Welfare Research. In M.C. Nussbaum and A.K. Sen, eds. *The Quality of Life*. Oxford: Clarendon Press, 67-83.

EU, 2000. *Presidency Conclusions*. Available from: www.ue.eu.int/en/info/eurocouncil/index.htm [accessed 23 January 2007].

Felce, D. and Perry, J., 1993. *Quality of Life: A Contribution to its Definition and Measurement*. Bangor: University of Wales.

Fine, B., 2000. *Social Capital versus Social Theory. Political Economy and Social Science at the Turn of the Millennium*. London: Routledge.

Fisch, H., 2002. Glück: Politische und ökonomische Einflüsse. In: A. Bellebaum, ed. *Glücksforschung: Eine Bestandsaufnahme*. Konstanz: UVK, 213-226.

Frederick, S. and Loewenstein, G., 1999. Hedonic Adaption. In: D. Kahnemann, E. Diener, N. Schwarz, eds. *Well-Being: The Foundations of Hedonic Psychology*. New York: Russell Sage Foundation, 302-329.

Freitag, M., 2003. Beyond Tocqueville: The Origins of Social Capital in Switzerland. *European Sociological Review*, 19, 217-232.

Frey, B. S. and Al-Roumi, A., 1999. Political Democracy and the Physical Quality of Life: Cross-National Evidence. *Social Indicators Research*, 33, 73-97.

Frey, B.S. and Stutzer, A., 2002. *Happiness and Economics. How the Economy and Institutions Affect Human Well-Being*. Princeton, NJ: Princeton University Press.

Frey, B.S. and Stutzer, A., 2005. Happiness Research: State and Prospects. *Review of Social Economy*, 62 (2), 207-228.

Frijda, N.H., 1999. Emotions and Hedonic Experience. In: D. Kahnemann, E. Diener, N. Schwarz, eds. *Well-Being: The Foundations of Hedonic Psychology*. New York: Russell Sage Foundation, 190-210.

Fukuyama, F., 1995. *Trust: The Social Virtues and the Creation of Prosperity*. New York: Free Press.

Fukuyama, F., 2000. Social Capital. In: S. Huntington and L.E. Harrison, ed. *Culture matters. How values shape human progress*. London: Basic Books, 98 – 111.

Gallie, D. and Russell, H., 1998. Unemployment and Life Satisfaction: A Cross-Cultural Comparison. *Archives European Sociology*, 34, 248-280.

Gallup, G.P., 1976. Human Needs and Satisfaction: A Global Survey. *Public Opinion Quarterly*, 40, 459-467.

Galtung, J., 1996. *Peace by Peaceful Means. Peace and Conflict, Development and Civilization*. London: Sage Publications.

Glatzer, W., 1992. Lebensqualität und subjektives Wohlbefinden. Ergebnisse sozialwissenschaftlicher Untersuchungen. In: A. Bellebaum, ed. *Glücksforschung: Eine Bestandsaufnahme*. Konstanz: UVK, 49 – 85.

Glatzer, W. and Zapf. W., 1984. Lebensqualität in der Bundesrepublik. In: W. Glatzer and W. Zapf, eds. *Lebensqualität in der Bundesrepublik. Objektive Lebensbedingungen und subjektives Wohlbefinden*. Frankfurt a.M.: Campus, 391-401.

Glatzer, W., 2004. Challenges for Quality of Life. In: W. Glatzer, S. von Below, and M. Stoffregen, ed. *Challenges for the Quality of Life in Contemporary Societies*. Dordrecht: Kluwer, 3 – 10.

Gossen, H. H., 1854. *Entwickelung der Gesetze des menschlichen Verkehrs und der daraus fließenden Regeln für menschliches Handeln*. Braunschweig: Vieweg und Sohn. Reprinted: 1987, Frankfurt am Main: Verlag Wirtschaft und Finanzen.

Graham, C., Eggers, A. and Sukhtankar, S., 2004. Does Happiness Pay? An Exploration Based on Panel Data from Russia. *Journal of Economic Behavior and Organization*, 55 (3), 319-342.

Graham, C. and Pettinato, S., 2002. Frustrated Achievers: Winners, Losers and Subjective Well-Being in New Market Economies. *Journal of Development Studies*, 38 (4), 100-140.

Granovetter, M., 1982. The Strength of Weak Ties. A Network Theory Revisited. In: P.V. Marsden. and L. Nan, eds. *Social Structure and Network Analysis*. London: Sage, 105-130.

Grinde, B., 2002a. Happiness in the Perspective of Evolutionary Psychology. In: *Journal of Happiness Studies*, 3, 331-354.

Grinde, B., 2002b. *Darwinian Happiness: Evolution as a Guide for Living and Understanding Human Behavior*. Princeton: Princeton University Press.

Grjebine, A., 2000. Tolérance Zéro sur les Routes. *Le Monde*, 26 May, p. 19.

Groot, W., Maassen van den Brink, H., van Praag, B., 2006. The Compensating Income Variation of Social Capital. Discussion Paper No. 2529. Bonn: IZA.

Grootaert, C., 2001. Social Capital: The Missing Link? In: P. Dekker, and E. Uslaner, eds. *Social Capital and Participation in Everyday Life*. London: Routledge.

Gundelach, P. and Kreiner, S., 2004. Happiness and Life Satisfaction in Advanced European Countries. *Cross-Cultural Research*, 38, 4, 359-386.

Gundelach, P., and Thorpe, L., 1997. Social Reflexivity, Democracy and New Types of Citizen Involvement in Denmark. In: J.W. Deth, ed. *Private Groups and Public Lives*. London: Routledge, 47-63.

Habich, R. and Zapf, W., 1994. Gesellschaftliche Dauerbeobachtung - Wohlfahrtssurveys: Instrument der Sozialberichterstattung. In: R. Hauser, N. Ott, G. Wagner, eds. *Mikroanalytische Grundlagen der Gesellschaftspolitik. Erhebungsverfahren, Analysemethoden und Mikrosimulation*. Berlin: Akademie, 13-37.

Hagerty, M., 2002. Declining Quality of Life Costs Governments Elections. Review of 13 OECD Countries. *Social Indicators Research*, 58, 383-402.

Hagerty, M., Cummins, R.A., Ferriss, A.L., Land, K., Michalos, A.C. and Peterson, M., 2001. Quality of Life Indexes for National Policy: Review and Agenda for Research. *Social Indicators Research*, 55, 1-96.

Hagerty, M. and Veenhoven, R., 2002. Why Social Policy Needs Subjective Indicators. *Social Indicators Research.*, 58, 33-45.

Hagerty, M. and Veenhoven, R., 2003. Wealth and Happiness Revisited. Growing Wealth of Nations Does Go with Greater Happiness. *Social Indicators Research*, 64, 1-27.

Hagerty, M., Vogel, J. and Møller, V., 2002. Introduction. In: M. Hagerty, J. Vogel and V. Møller, eds. *Assessing Quality of Life and Living Conditions to Guide National Policy: The State of the Art*. Dordrecht: Kluwer, 1-11.

Haller, M. and Hadler, M., 2004. Happiness as an Expression of Freedom and Self-Determination. A Comparative Multilevel Analysis. W. Glatzer, S. von Below, and M. Stoffregen, ed. *Challenges for the Quality of Life in Contemporary Societies*. Dordrecht: Kluwer, 207 – 231.

Hambleton, R. K. and Patsula, L., 1998. Adapting Tests for Use in Multiple Languages and Cultures. *Social Indicators Research*, 45, 153-171.

Hanifan, L. J., 1916. The Rural School and Community Center. *Annals of the American Academy of Political and Social Science*, 67, 130-138.

Harpham, T., Grant, E. and Thomas, E., 2002. Measuring Social Capital within Health Surveys: Key Issues. *Health Policy and Planning*, 17 (1), 106-111.

Harpham, T., Grant, E. and Rodriguez, C., 2004. Mental Health and Social Capital in Cali, Colombia. *Social Science and Medicine*, 58 (11), 2267-2277.

Headey, B. and Wearing, A., 1988. The Sense of Relative Superiority – Central to Well-Being. *Social Indicators Research*, 20, 497-516.

Headey, B. and Wearing, A., 1989. Personality, Life Events, and Subjective Well-Being: Toward a Dynamic Equilibrium Model. *Journal of Personality and Social Psychology*, 57, 731-739.

Headey, B. and Wearing, A., 1992. *Understanding Happiness: A Theory of Subjective Well-Being*. Longman Cheshire, Melbourne.

Helliwell, J. F., 2001. Social Capital, the Economy and Well-Being. In: K. Banting, A. Sharpe and F. St-Hilaire, eds. *The Review of Economic Performance and Social Progress*. Montreal: Institute for Research on Public Policy and Centre for the Study of Living Standards, 43–60.

Helliwell, John F., 2003. How's Life? Combining Individual and National Variables to Explain Subjective Well-Being. *Economic Modelling*, 20 (2), 331-60.

Helliwell, J. F., 2004. *Well-Being and Social Capital: Does Suicide Pose a Puzzle?* NBER Working Paper 10896. Cambridge MA: National Bureau of Economic Research.

Helliwell, J. F., 2006. Well-Being, Social Capital and Public Policy: What's New? *Economic Journal*, 116 (510), C34-C45.

Helliwell, J.F. and Huang, H., 2006. *How's Your Government? International Evidence Linking Good Government and Well-Being*. NBER Working Paper 11988. Cambridge MA: National Bureau of Economic Research.

Helliwell, J. F. and Putnam, R. D., 2004. The Social Context of Well-Being. In: F. A. Huppert, B. Kaverne and N. Baylis, eds. *The Science of Well-Being*. London: Oxford University Press, 435–459.

Hettlage, R., 2002. Generative Glückserfahrungen: Biographien, Kohorten und Mentalitäten. In: A. Bellebaum, ed. *Glücksforschung: Eine Bestandsaufnahme*. Konstanz: UVK, 129-156.

Hirsch, F., 1976. *The Social Limits to Growth*. Cambridge, MA: Harvard University Press.

Holtgrave, D.R. and Crosby, R.A., 2004. Social Determinants of Tuberculosis Rates in the United States. *American Journal of Preventive Medicine*, 26, 156-62.

Hudler, M. and Richter, R., 2002. Cross-National Comparison of the Quality of Life in Europe: Inventory of Surveys and Methods. *Social Indicators Research*, 58, 217-228.

Hudler-Seitzberger, M., 2004. Comparative Survey Questions on Quality of Life: The Dynamic Information Centre. In: W. Glatzer, S. von Below, and M. Stoffregen, ed. *Challenges for the Quality of Life in Contemporary Societies*. Dordrecht: Kluwer, 91 – 106.

Inglehart, R., 1990. *Culture Shift in Advanced Industrial Society*. Princeton: Princeton University Press.

Inglehart, R., 1997. *Modernization and Postmodernization: Cultural, Economic and Political Change in 43 Societies*. Princeton: Princeton University Press.

Inglehart, R., 2000. Globalization and Postmodern Values. In: *The Washington Quarterly*, 23, 215–228.

Inglehart, R. and Klingemann, H.-D., 2000. Genes, Culture, Democracy and Happiness. In: E. Diener and E.M. Suh, eds. *Culture and Subjective Well-Being*. Cambridge, MA: Bradford, 165-184.

Inglehart, R. and Rabier, J.R., 1984a. Du Bonheur...Ou Comment les Aspirations S'Adaptent aux Situations. *Futuribles*, 81 (9), 29-58.

Inglehart, R. and Rabier, J.R., 1984b. Du Bonheur...Sentiment Personnel et Norme Culturelle. *Futuribles*, 81 (10), 3-28.

Inglehart, R. and Rabier, J.-R., 1986. Aspirations Adapt to Situations - But Why Are the Belgians so Much Happier than the French? A Cross-Cultural Analysis of the Subjective Quality of Life. In: F.M. Andrews, ed. *Research on the Quality of Life*. Ann Arbor: University of Michigan, 1-56.

Inglehart, R. and Welzel, C., 2005. *Modernization, Cultural Change and Democracy. The Human Development Sequence*. Cambridge: Cambridge University Press.

Isham, J., Kelly, T. and Ramaswamy, S., 2002. Social Capital and Well-being in Developing Countries: An Introduction. In: J. Isham, T. Kelly and S. Ramaswamy, eds. *Social Capital and Economic Development: Well-Being in Developing Countries*. Northampton, MA: Edward Elgar, 3-17.

Jacobs, J., 1961. *The Death and Life of Great American Cities*. New York: Random House.

Jayawardena, L. 1993. Foreword. In: M. Nussbaum and A. Sen, eds. *The Quality of Life*. Oxford: Clarendon Press, III-IV.

Kahnemann, D., 1999. Objective Happiness. In: D. Kahnemann, E. Diener, N. Schwarz, eds. *Well-Being: The Foundations of Hedonic Psychology*. New York: Russell Sage Foundation, 3-25.

Kasser, T. and Ryan, R. M., 1993. A Dark Side of the American Dream: Correlates of Financial Success as a Central Life Aspiration. *Journal of Personality and Social Psychology*, 65, 410-422.

Kawachi, I. and Berkman, L.F., 2003. *Neighborhoods and Health*. New York: Oxford University Press.

Kawachi, I., and Kennedy, B.P., 1999. Income Inequality and Health: Pathways and Mechanisms. *Health Services Research*, 34, 215.

Kawachi, I., Kennedy, B. P. and Glass, R., 1999. Social Capital and Self-Rated Health: A Contextual Analysis. *American Journal of Public Health*, 89, 1187-1193.

Kawachi, I., Kennedy, B. P., Lochner, K. and Prothrow-Stith, D., 1997. Social Capital, Income Inequality and Mortality. *American Journal of Public Health*, 87 (9), 1491-1498.

Kennedy, B. P., Kawachi, I., Prothrow-Stith, D., Lochner, K. and Gupta, V., 1998. Social Capital, Income Inequality and Firearm Violent Crime. *Social Science and Medicine*, 47, 7-17.

Kennelly, B., O'Shea, E. and Garvey, E., 2003. Social Capital, Life Expectancy and Mortality: A Cross-National Examination. *Social Science and Medicine*, 56, 2367-2377.

Keck, W. and Delhey, J., 2004. Subjective Well-Being. In: European Foundation for the Improvement of Living and Working Conditions, ed. *Quality of Life in Europe. First Results of a New Pan-European Survey*. Dublin: Eurofund, 63-70.

Kenny, C., 1999. Does Growth Cause Happiness, or Does Happiness Cause Growth? *Kyklos*, 52 (1), 3-26.

Kenny, C., 2005. Does Development Make You Happy? Subjective Well-Being and Economic Growth in Developing Countries. *Social Indicators Research*, 73, 199-220.

Klitgaard, R., 1990. *Tropical Gangsters*. New York: Basic Books.

Kitayama, S. and Markus, H. R., 2000. The Pursuit of Happiness and the Realization of Sympathy: Cultural Patterns of Self, Social Relations, and Well-Being. In: E. Diener and E.M. Suh, eds. *Culture and Subjective Well-Being*. Cambridge, MA: Bradford, 113-162.

Knack, S., 2001. Trust, Associational Life and Economic Performance. In: J.F. Helliwell, ed. *The Contribution of Human and Social Capital to Sustained Economic Growth and Well-Being*. Ottawa: HDRC, 172–202.

Knack, S. and Keefer, P., 1997. Does Social Capital Have an Economic Payoff? A Cross-Country Investigation. *Quaterly Journal of Economics*, 112 (4), 1251 – 88.

Krause, P., 2004. Die Bedeutung von Vergleichsstandards und Vergleichsprozessen für die Erklärung des subjektiven Wohlbefindens. In: *Conference on „Subjektives Wohlbefinden und subjektive Indikatoren: Konzepte, Daten und Analysen", 2-3 December 2004*. Mannheim: ZUMA.

Ladd, E., 1996. The Data Just Don't Show Erosion of America's Social Capital. *Public Perspective*, 7, 4-22.

Land, K. C., 1983. Social Indicators. *Annual Review of Sociology*, 9, 1-26.

Land, K.C., 2000. Social Indicators. In: E. F. Borgatta and R. V. Montgomery, eds., *Encyclopedia of Sociology*, Revised Edition. New York: Macmillan.

Lane, R. E., 1991. *The Market Experience*. New York: Cambridge University Press.

Lane, R.E., 1996. Quality of Life and Quality of Persons: A New Role for Government. In: A. Offer, ed. *In Pursuit of the Quality of Life*. Oxford: Oxford University Press, 256-293.

Lane, R.E., 2000. *The Loss of Happiness in Market Democracies*. New Haven: Yale University Press.

Larsen, R.J. and Frederickson, B.L., 1999. Measurement Issues in Emotion Research. In: D. Kahnemann, E. Diener, N. Schwarz, eds. *Well-Being: The Foundations of Hedonic Psychology*. New York: Russell Sage Foundation, 40-60.

Layard, R., 2005. *Happiness: Lessons from a New Science*. New York: Penguin.

Lewis, D. and Weigert, A., 1985. Trust as a Social Reality. *Social Forces*, 63 (3), 967-85.

Lindström M., 2004. Social Capital, the Miniaturisation of Community and Self-Reported Global and Psychological Health. *Social Science and Medicine*, 59, 595-607.

Lochner, K.A., Kawachi, I., Brennan, R.T. and Buka, S.L., 2003. Social Capital and Neighborhood Mortality Rates in Chicago. *Social Science and Medicine*, 56, 1797-1805.

Lont, A. and Dronkers, J., 2004. Parental Divorce and the Well-being of Adolescent Children. Changes between 1984-1999 in the Netherlands. In: W. Glatzer, S. von Below, and M. Stoffregen, ed. *Challenges for the Quality of Life in Contemporary Societies*. Dordrecht: Kluwer, 249-270.

Loury, G. C., 1977. A Dynamic Theory of Racial Income Differences. In: P.A. Wallace and A. Le Mund, eds. *Women, Minorities, and Employment Discrimination*. Lexington, MA: Lexington Books.

Lucas, R.E., 2007. Adaptation and the Set-Point Model of Subjective Well-Being: Does Happiness Change after Major Life Events? *Current Directions in Psychological Science*, 16 (2), 75-79.

Lykken, D. and Tellegen, A., 1996. Happiness is a Stochastic Phenomenon. *Psychological Science*, 7, 186–189.

Lyubomirsky, S. and Lepper, H., 1999. A Measure of Subjective Happiness. Preliminary Reliability and Construct Validation. *Social Indicators Research*, 46, 137-155.

Max-Neef, M., 1995. Economic Growth and Quality of Life: A Threshold Hypothesis. *Ecological Economics*, 15, 115-118.

Maslow, A.H., 1981. *Motivation und Persönlichkeit*. Reinbek: Rowohlt.

Michalos, A. C., 1985. Multiple Discrepancies Theory (MDT). *Social Indicators Research*, 16, 347-413.

Michalos, A. C., 1986. Job Satisfaction, Marital Satisfaction, and the Quality of Life: A Review and a Preview. In: F.M. Andrews, ed. *Research on the Quality of Life*. Ann Arbor: University of Michigan, 57-83.

Michalos, A. C., 1990. The Impact of Trust on Business, International Security and the Quality of Life. *Journal of Business Ethics*, 9, 619-638.

Michalos, A.C., 1991. *Global Report on Student Well-Being. Volume 1: Life Satisfaction and Happiness*. New York: Springer.

Michalos, A. C., 1992. Subjective Well-Being: An Interdisciplinary Perspective. *Social Indicators Research*, 26, 199-203.

Michalos, A.C., 2001. Multiple Discrepancies Theory (MDT). *Social Indicators Research*, 53, 189-222.

Michalos, A.C., 2003. *Essays on the Quality of Life*. Dordrecht: Kluwer.

Mishan, E.J., 1967. *The Costs of Economic Growth*. London: Staples.

Mohr, G., 1997. *Erwerbslosigkeit, Arbeitsplatzunsicherheit und psychische Befindlichkeit*. Frankfurt am Main: Lang.

Mulgan, G., 2003. Vom Staat und vom Glück. *Die Zeit*, 11 March, p. 13.

Myers, D.G., 1999. Close Relationships and Quality of Life. In: D. Kahnemann, E. Diener, N. Schwarz, eds. *Well-Being: The Foundations of Hedonic Psychology*. New York: Russell Sage Foundation, 374-391.

Myers, D.G., 2000. The Funds, Friends, and Faith of Happy People. *American Psychologist*, 55 (1), 56-67.

Myers, D. G. and Diener, E., 1995. Who is Happy? *Psychological Science*, 6, 10-19.

Narayan, D., 2002. Bonds and Bridges: Social Capital and Poverty. In: J. Isham, T. Kelly and S. Ramaswamy, eds. *Social Capital and Economic Development: Well-Being in Developing Countries*. Northampton: Edward Elgar, 58-81.

Narayan, D. and Cassidy, M., 2001. A Dimensional Approach to Measuring Social Capital: Development and Validation of Social Capital Inventory. *Current Sociology*, 49 (2), 49-93.

Narayan, D. and Pritchett, L., 2000. Social Capital: Evidence and Implications. In: P. Dasgupta and I. Serageldin, eds. *Social Capital: A Multifaceted Perspective*. Washington D.C.: World Bank, 325-424.

Nieboer, A. and Lindenberg, S., 2002. Substitution, Buffers and Subjective Well-Being: A Hierarchical Approach. In: E. Gullone and R.A. Cummins, eds. *The Universality of Subjective Well-Being Indicators*. Dordrecht: Kluwer, 175-189.

Neumark, D. and Postlewaite, A., 1998. Relative Income Concerns and the Rise in Married Women's Employment. *Journal of Public Economics*, 70 (1), 157-83.

Nickerson, C., Schwarz, N., Kahnemann, D. and Diener, E., 2003. Zeroing in on the Dark Side of the American Dream: A Closer Look at the Negative Consequences of the Goal for Financial Success. *Psychological Science*, 14 (6), 531-536.

Nolen-Hoeksema, S. and Rusting, C.L., 1999. Gender Differences in Well-Being. In: D. Kahnemann, E. Diener, N. Schwarz, eds. *Well-Being: The Foundations of Hedonic Psychology*. New York: Russell Sage Foundation, 330-351.

Noll, H.-H., 1997. Wohlstand, Lebensqualität und Wohlbefinden in den Ländern der Europäischen Union. In: S. Hradil and S. Immerfall, eds. *Die westeuropäischen Gesellschaften im Vergleich*. Opladen: Leske and Budrich, 431-474.

Noll, H.-H., 1999. *Konzepte der Wohlfahrtsentwicklung: Lebensqualität und „neue" Wohlfahrtskonzepte.* EuReporting Working Paper No. 3. Mannheim: ZUMA.

Noll, H.-H., 2000. *Social Indicators and Social Reporting: The International Experience.* Available from: http://www.ccsd.ca/noll1.html [accessed on 14 Feb. 2007].

Noll, H.-H., 2004. Social Indicators and Quality of Life Research: Background, Achievements and Current Trends. In: N. Genov, ed. *Advances in Sociological Knowledge. Over Half a Century, Vol. 1.* Wiesbaden: VS Verlag für Sozialwissenschaften, 151-181.

Noll, H.-H. and Zapf, W., 1994. Social Indicators Research: Societal Monitoring and Social Reporting. In: I. Borg and P. P. Mohler, eds. *Trends and Perspectives in Empirical Social Research.* New York: de Gruyter, 1-16.

Nordhaus, W.D. and Tobin, J., 1972. Is Growth Obsolete? *National Bureau of Economic Research General Series*, 96, 1-80.

Nozick, R., 1989. *The Examined Life: Philosophical Meditations.* New York: Simon and Schuster.

Nussbaum, M.C., 1993. Non-Relative Virtues. An Aristotelian Approach. In: M. Nussbaum and A. Sen, eds. *The Quality of Life.* New York: Oxford University Press, 242-277.

Nussbaum, M.C. and Sen, A., 1993. Introduction. In: M.C. Nussbaum and A. Sen, eds. *The Quality of Life.* New York: Oxford University Press, 1-8.

OECD, 2001. *The Well-Being of Nations: The Role of Human and Social Capital.* Paris: OECD.

Offer, A., 1996. Introduction. In: A. Offer, ed. *In pursuit of the Quality of Life.* Oxford: Oxford University Press, 1-17.

Offer, A., 2000. *Economic Welfare Measurements and Human Well-Being.* Discussion Papers in Economic and Social History, no. 34. Oxford: Oxford University.

Offer, A., 2006. *The Challenge of Affluence: Self-Control and Well-Being in the United States and Britain since 1950*. Oxford: Oxford University Press.

Oishi, S., 2000. Goals as Cornerstones of Subjective Well-Being: Linking Individuals and Cultures. In: D. Kahnemann, E. Diener, N. Schwarz, eds. *Well-Being: The Foundations of Hedonic Psychology*. New York: Russell Sage Foundation, 87-112.

Oishi, S. and Diener, E., 2001. Goals, Culture, and Subjective Well-Being. *Personality and Social Psychology Bulletin*, 27 (12), 1674-1682.

Oishi, S., Diener, E., Lucas, R.E. and Suh, E.M., 1999. Cross-Cultural Variations in Predictors of Life Satisfation: Perspectives from Needs and Values. *Personality and Social Psychology Bulletin*, 25, 980-991.

Ostroot, N. M. and Snyder, W.W., 1985. Measuring Cultural Bias in a Cross-National Study, *Social Indicators Research*, 17, 243-251.

Oswald, A.J., 1997. Happiness and Economic Performance. *Economic Journal*, 107, 1815-1831.

Ouweneel, P. and Veenhoven, R., 1991. Cross-National Differences in Happiness: Cultural Bias or Social Quality. In: N. Bleichrodt and P.J.D. Drenth, eds. *Contemporary Issues in Cross-Cultural Psychology*. Amsterdam: Swets and Zetlinger.

Phillips, A.W., 1958. The Relationship between Unemployment and the Rate of Change of Money Wages in the United Kingdom 1861-1957. *Economica*, 25, 283-299.

Pavot, W. and Diener, E., 1993. Review of the Satisfaction with Life Scale. *Psychological Assessment*, 5, 164-172.

Pollack, C.E. and von dem Knesebeck, O., 2004. Social Capital and Health among the Aged: Comparisons between the United States and Germany. *Health Place*, 10 (4), 383-391.

Poortinga, W., 2006. Social Capital: An individual or Collective Resource for Health? *Social Science and Medicine*, 62 (2), 292-302.

Portes, A., 2000. Social Capital: Its origins and Applications in Modern Sociology. In: Lesser, E., ed. *Knowledge and Social Capital*. Boston: Butterworth-Heinemann, 43-69.

Power, M.J., Bullinger, M. and the WHOQOL Group (2002). The Universality of Quality of Life: An Empirical Approach Using the WHOQOL. In: E. Gullone and R.A. Cummins, eds. *The Universality of Subjective Well-Being Indicators*. Social Indicators Research Book Series, Volume 16. Dordrecht: Kluwer, 129-150.

Pugno, M., 2005. The Happiness Paradox: A Formal Explanation from Psycho-Economics. Technical Report 1, *Economia.* Available from: http://www.econo.economia.unitn.it/new/pubblicazioni/papers/ 1_05_pugno.pdf [accessed 15 February 2007].

Putnam, H., 1993. Objectivity and the Science-Ethics Distinction. In: M. Nussbaum and A. Sen, eds. *The Quality of Life*. New York: Oxford University Press, 143-164.

Putnam, R. D., Leonardi, R. and Nanetti, R., 1993. *Making Democracy Work: Civic Traditions in Modern Italy*. Princeton University Press.

Putnam, R. D., 2000. *Bowling Alone: The Collapse and Revival of American Community*. New York: Simon and Schuster.

Putnam, R. D., 2001 (ed.). *Gesellschaft und Gemeinsinn.* Gütersloh: Bertelsmann.

Ratzlaff, C., Matsumoto, D., Kouznetsova, N., Raroque, J. and Ray, R., 2000. Individual Psychological Culture and Subjective Well-Being. In: E. Diener and E.M. Suh, eds. *Culture and Subjective Well-Being*. Cambridge, MA: Bradford, 37-60.

Rapley, M., 2003. *Quality of Life Research*. London: Sage Publications.

Requena, F., 2003. Social Capital, Satisfaction and Quality of Life in the Workplace. *Social Indicators Research*, 61 (3), 331-360.

Rodrik, D., 1999. Where Did All the Growth Go? External Shocks, Social Conflict, and Growth Collapses. *Journal of Economic Growth*. 4 (4). 385-412.

Rojas, Y. and Carlson, P., 2005. The Stratification of Social Capital and its Consequences for Self-Rated Health in Taganrog, Russia. *Social Science and Medicine*, 62 (11), 2732-2741.

Ross, C.E. and Mirowsky, J., 2002. Family Relationships, Social Support and Subjective Life Expectancy. *Journal of Health and Social Behavior*, 43 (4), 469-489.

Ross, C.E., Reynolds, J. and Geis, K., 2000. The Contingent Meaning of Neighborhood Stability for Residents' Psychological Well-being. *American Sociological Review*, 65, 581-597.

Rotter, J.B., 1980. Interpersonal Trust, Trustworthiness, and Gullibility. *American Psychologist*, 35, 1-7.

Samuelson, R., 1995. *The Good Life and its Discontents*. New York: Times.

Sandvik, E., Diener, E. and Seidlitz, L., 1993. Subjective Well-Being: The Convergence and Stability of Self-Report and Non-Self-Report Measures. *Journal of Personality*, 61, 318-342.

Saris, W.E., 2001. What Influences Subjective Well-Being in Russia? *Journal of Happiness Studies*, 2, 137-146.

Saris, W.E., van Wijk, T. and Scherpenzeel, A.C., 1998. Validity and Reliability of Subjective Social Indicators: The Effect of Different Measures of Association. *Social Indicators Research*, 45, 173-199.

Scanlon, T., 1993. Value, Desire, and Quality of Life. In: M. Nussbaum and A. Sen, eds. *The Quality of Life*. New York: Oxford University Press, 185-207.

Scherpenzeel, A.C. and Saris, W.E., 1997. The Validity and Reliability of Survey Questions: A Meta-Analysis of MTMM Studies. *Sociological Methods and Research*, 25 (3), 341-367.

Schudson, M., 1996. What If Civic Life Didn't Die? *American Prospect*, 25, 17 – 20.

Schumacher, J., Klaiberg, A. and Brähler, E. 2003. Diagnostik von Lebensqualität und Wohlbefinden - Eine Einführung. In: J. Schumacher, A. Klaiberg, E. Brähler, eds. *Diagnostische Verfahren zu Lebensqualität und Wohlbefinden*. Göttingen: Hogrefe, 9-24.

Schwartz, S.H. and Melech, G., 2000. National Differences in Micro and Macro Worry: Social, Economic, and Cultural Explanations. In: E. Diener and E.M. Suh, eds. *Culture and Subjective Well-Being*. Cambridge, MA: Bradford, 219-256.

Schwarz, N. and Strack, F., 1999. Reports of Subjective Well-Being: Judgmental Processes and Their Methodological Implications. In: D. Kahnemann, E. Diener, N. Schwarz, eds. *Well-Being: The Foundations of Hedonic Psychology*. New York: Russell Sage Foundation, 61-84.

Schyns, P., 1998. Cross-national Differences in Happiness: Economic and Cultural Factors Explored. *Social Indicators Research*, 43, 3-26.

Seligmann, M., 2002. *Authentic Happiness: Using the New Positive Psychology to Realize Your Potential for Lasting Fulfilment*. New York: Free Press.

Sellerberg, A.-M., 1982. On Modern Confidence. *Acta Sociologica*, 25 (1), 39-48.

Sen, A., 1993. Capability and Well-Being. In: M.C. Nussbaum and A. Sen, eds. *The Quality of Life*. New York: Oxford University Press, 30-53.

Segall, M.H., Dasen, D.R., Berry, J.W. and Poortinga, Y.H., 1990. *Human Behavior in Global Perspective*. New York: Pergamon Press.

Shafir, E., Diamond, P. and Tversky, A., 1997. Money Illusion. *The Quarterly Journal of Economics*. 62, 341-374.

Shiller, R.J., 1997. *Public Resistance to Indexation: A Puzzle*. Washington D.C.: Brookings Institution Press.

Sirgy, J., 2001. *Handbook of Quality-of-Life Research. An Ethical Marketing-Perspective*. Dordrecht: Kluwer.

Sirgy, J., Michalos, A.C., Abbott, L. F., Richard E., Pavot, W. and Patrick, D., 2006. The Quality of Life (QOL) Research Movement: Past, Present, and Future. *Social Indicators Research*, 76, 363-377.

Skrabski, Á., Kopp, M. and Kawachi, I., 2004. Social Capital and Collective Efficacy in Hungary: Cross-Sectional Associations with Middle-Aged Female and Male Mortality Rates. *Journal of Epidemiology and Community Health*, 58, 340–345.

Stewart, F., 1996. Basic Needs, Capabilities, and Human Development. In: A. Offer, ed. *In pursuit of the Quality of Life*. Oxford: Oxford University Press, 46-65.

Stones, M.J., Hadjistavropoulos, T., Tuuko, H. and Kozma, A., 1995. Happiness has Traitlike and Statelike Properties: A reply to Veenhoven. *Social Indicators Research*, 36, 129-144.

Strack, F., Argyle, M., and Schwarz, N., 1991. *Subjective Well-Being: An Interdisciplinary Perspective*. Oxford: Pergamon.

Stutzer, A., 2004. The Role of Income Aspirations in Individual Happiness. *Journal of Economic Behavior and Organization*, 54 (1), 89-110.

Subramanian, S.V., Kawachi, I. and Kennedy, B.P., 2001. Does the State You Live in Make a Difference? Multilevel Analysis of Self-Rated Health in the US. *Social Science and Medicine*, 53, 9-19.

Sudman, S., Bradburn, N. M. and Schwarz, N., 1996. *Thinking About Questions: The Application of Cognitive Processes to Survey Methodology*. San Francisco: Jossey-Bass Publishers.

Sudman, S., Greeley, A. M., and Pinto, L. J., 1967. The Use of Self-Administered Questionnaires. In: S. Sudman, ed. *Reducing the Cost of Surveys*. Chicago: Aldine, 46-57.

Suh, E. M., 2000. Self, the Hyphen between Culture and Subjective Well-Being. In: E. Diener and E.M. Suh, eds. *Culture and Subjective Well-Being*. Cambridge, MA: Bradford, 63-86.

Suh, E., Diener, E., Oishi, S., and Triandis, H.C., 1998. The Shifting Basis of Life Satisfaction Judgments Across Cultures: Emotions Versus Norms. In: *Journal of Personality and Social Psychology*, 74, 1998 (2), 482-493.

Taylor, C., 1993. Explanation and Practical Reason. In: M. Nussbaum and A. Sen, eds. *The Quality of Life*. New York: Oxford University Press, 208-241.

Tellegen, A., Lykken, D., Bouchard, T., Wilcox, K., Segal, N. and Rich, S., 1988. Personality Similarity in Twins Reared Apart and Separately. *Journal of Personality and Social Psychology*, 54, 1031-1039.

Temple, J., 2000. *Growth Effects of Education and Social Capital in the OECD Countries*. Working Paper no. 263. Paris: Economic Department, OECD.

Thomas, W.I. and. Thomas, D. S., 1928. *The Child in America: Behavior Problems and Programs*. New York: Knopf.

Tiberius, V., 2004. Cultural Differences and Philosophical Accounts of Well-Being. *Journal of Happiness Studies*, 5 (3), 219-222.

Tönnies, F., 2005 [1887]. *Gemeinschaft und Gesellschaft*. Darmstadt: Wissenschaftliche Buchgesellschaft.

Triandis, H., 2000. Cultural Syndromes and Subjective Well-Being. In: E. Diener and E.M. Suh, eds. *Culture and Subjective Well-Being*. Cambridge, MA: Bradford, 13-36.

Tversky, A. and Griffin, D., 1991. Endowment and Contrast in Judgements of Well-Being. In: F. Strack, M. Argyle and N. Schwarz, eds. *Subjective Well-Being: An Interdisciplinary Perspective*. New York: Plenum Press, 101-118.

United Nations, 1994. *Information on Social Development Publications and Indicators in the United Nations System*. Working Paper No. 7. New York: United Nations Publications.

United Nations Development Program (UNDP), 1990. *Human Development Report*. New York: Oxford University Press.

United Nations World Institute for Development Economics Research (UNU-WIDER), 2005. *World Income Inequality Database Version 2.0a*, June 2005. Available from: http://www.wider.unu.edu/wiid/wiid.htm [accessed on 17 March 2007].

United States Congress, 1776. *Declaration of Independence*. Philadelphia: John Dunlap.

Utsey, S. O., Bolden, M. A., Brown, C. F. and Chae, M. H., 2001. Assessing Quality of Life in the Context of Culture. In: L.A. Suzuki, J. G. Ponterotto and P.J. Meller, eds. *Handbook of Multicultural Assessment: Clinical, Psychological, and Educational Applications*. San Francisco: Jossey-Bass, 191-211.

Uusitalo, H., 1994. Social Statistics and Social Reporting in the Nordic Countries. In: P. Flora, F. Kraus, H.-H. Noll and F. Rothenbacher, eds. *Social Statistics and Social Reporting in and for Europe*. Bonn: Informationszentrum Sozialwissenschaften, 99-120.

van Praag, B.M.S. and Frijters, P., 1999. The Measurement of Welfare and Well-Being. The Leyden Approach. In: D. Kahnemann, E. Diener, N. Schwarz, eds. *Well-Being: The Foundations of Hedonic Psychology*. New York: Russell Sage Foundation, 413-433.

Veenhoven, R., 1987. Cultural Bias in Ratings of Perceived Life Quality. *Social Indicators Research*, 18, 329-334.

Veenhoven R., 1989. National Wealth and Individual Happiness. In: K.G. Grunert and M. Olander, eds. *Understanding Economic Behavior*, Kluwer, pp 9-32.

Veenhoven, R., 1991. Questions on Happiness: Classical Topics, Modern Answers, Blind Spots. In: F. Strack, M. Argyle and N. Schwarz, eds. *Subjective Well-Being: An Interdisciplinary Perspective*. New York: Plenum Press, 7-26.

Veenhoven, R., 1993. *Happiness in Nations. Subjective Appreciation of Life in 56 Nations 1946-1992*. RISBO, Studies in Sociale en Culturele Verandering. Rotterdam: Erasmus University.

Veenhoven, R., 1994. Is Happiness a Trait? Tests of the Theory that a Better Society Does Not Make People any Happier. *Social Indicators Research*, 32, 101-160.

Veenhoven, R., 1996a. Happy Life-Expectancy. A Comprehensive Measure of Quality-of-Life in Nations. *Social Indicators Research*, 39, 1–58.

Veenhoven, R., 1996b. The Study of Life-Satisfaction. In: W.E. Saris, R. Veenhoven, A.C. Scherpenzeel and B. Bunting, eds. *A Comparative Study of Satisfaction with Life in Europe*. Budapest: Eötvös University Press, 11-48.

Veenhoven, R., 1997. Progrés dans la Compréhension du Bonheur. *Revue Québécoise de Psychologie*, 18, 29-74.

Veenhoven, R., 2000. Freedom and Happiness: A Comparative Study in Forty-Four Nations in the Early 1990s. In: E. Diener and E.M. Suh, eds. *Culture and Subjective Well-Being*. Cambridge, MA: Bradford, 257-288.

Veenhoven, R., 2002. Why Social Policy Needs Subjective Indicators. *Social Indicators Research*, 58, 33-45.

Veenhoven, R., 2004. *Subjective Measures of Well-Being*. New York: United Nations University.

Veenhoven, R., 2004. World Database of Happiness: Continuous Register of Research on Subjective Appreciation of Life. In: W. Glatzer, S. von Below, and M. Stoffregen, ed. *Challenges for the Quality of Life in Contemporary Societies*. Dordrecht: Kluwer, 75–90.

Veenhoven, R. and Ouweneel, P., 1995. Livability of the Welfare State, Length of Life and Appreciation of Life in Nations Varying in State Welfare Effort. *Social Indicators Research*, 36, 1–48.

Vemuri, A.W. and Costanza, R., 2006. The Role of Human, Social, Built, and Natural Capital in Explaining Life Satisfaction at the Country Level: Toward a National Well-Being Index (NWI). *Ecological Economics,* 58, 1, 119-133.

Veenstra, G., 2000. Social Capital, SES and Health: An Individual-Level Analysis. *Social Science and Medicine*, 50, 619-629.

Vittersø, J., Roysamb, E. and Diener, E., 2002. The Concept of Life Satisfaction Across Cultures: Exploring its Diverse Meaning and Relation to Economics Wealth. In: E. Gullone and R.A. Cummins, eds. *The Universality of Subjective Well-Being Indicators*. Social Indicators Research Book Series, Volume 16. Dordrecht: Kluwer, 81-104.

von dem Knesebeck, O., Dragano, N. and Siegrist, J., 2005. Social Capital and Self-Rated Health in 21 European Countries. *GMS Psycho-Social-Medicine*, 2, Doc02.

Walker, A. and van der Maesen, L., 2004. Social Quality and Quality of Life. In: W. Glatzer, S. von Below, and M. Stoffregen, ed. *Challenges for the Quality of Life in Contemporary Societies*. Dordrecht: Kluwer, 13-32.

Walzer, M., 1993. Objectivity and Social Meaning. In: M. Nussbaum and A. Sen, eds. *The Quality of Life*. New York: Oxford University Press, 165-177.

Warr, P., 1999. Well-Being and the Workplace. In: D. Kahnemann, E. Diener, N. Schwarz, eds. *Well-Being: The Foundations of Hedonic Psychology*. New York: Russell Sage Foundation, 392-412.

Watson, D., Clark, L.A. and Tellegen, A., 1988. Development and Validation of Brief Measures of Positive and Negative Affect: The PANAS Scales. *Journal of Personality and Social Psychology*, 54, 1063-1070.

Weller, I., 1996. *Lebenszufriedenheit im europäischen Vergleich*. Discussion Paper FS-III 96-402. Berlin: WZB.

Wilson, W., 1967. Correlates of Avowed Happiness. *Psychological Bulletin*, 67, 294–306.

Wilkinson, R. G., 1996. *Unhealthy Societies: The Afflictions of Inequality*. London: Routledge.

Winter, I., 2000. Major Themes and Debates in the Social Capital Literature: The Australian Connection. In: I. Winter, ed. *Social Capital and Public Policy in Australia*. Melbourne: Australian Institute of Family Studies, 17–42.

Wolfson, M., Kaplan, G., Lynch, J., Ross, N., Backlund, E., Gravelle, H. and Wilkinson, R.G., 1999. Relation Between Income Inequality and Mortality: Empirical Demonstration. *British Medical Journal*, 319, 953-957.

Woolcock, M., 1998. Social Capital and Economic Development: Towards a Theoretical Synthesis and Policy Framework. *Theory and Society*, 27, 151 – 208.

Woolcock, M., 1999. Managing Risk, Shocks, and Opportunity in Developing Economies: The Role of Social Capital. In: G. Ranis, ed. *Dimensions of Development*. New Haven, CT: Yale Center for International and Area Studies, 197-212.

Woolcock, M. and Narayan, D., 2000. Social Capital: Implications for Development Theory, Research, and Policy." *World Bank Research Observer*, 15 (2), 225-50.

Woolcock, M., (2001). The Place of Social Capital in Understanding Social and Economic Outcomes. In: J.F. Helliwell, ed. *The Contribution of Human and Social Capital to Sustained Economic Growth and Well-Being. OECD/HRDC Conference, Quebec, 19-21 March 2000*. Ottawa: HRDC, 65–88.

World Bank, 2000. *World Development Report 2000/2001: Attacking Poverty*. New York: Oxford University Press.

World Bank, 2004. *Measuring Social Capital: An Integrated Questionnaire*. Washington D.C.: The World Bank.

World Bank, 2006. *World Development Indicators [CD-ROM]*. Washington D.C.: The World Bank.

World Values Survey Group, 2006. *Introduction to the World Values Survey*. Available from: http://www.worldvaluessurvey.org [accessed 12 Jan. 2007].

Yip, W., Subramanian, S.V., Mitchell, A.D., Lee, D., Wang, J. and Kawachi, I., 2006. Does Social Capital Enhance Health and Well-Being? Evidence from Rural China. *Social Science and Medicine*, 64, 35–49.

Zak, P.J. and Knack, P., 1998. *Trust and Growth*. IRIS Working Paper 219. College Park, MD: University of Maryland.

Zapf, W., 1984. Individuelle Wohlfahrt: Lebensbedingungen und wahrgenommene Lebensqualität. In: W. Glatzer and W. Zapf, eds. *Lebensqualität in der Bundesrepublik*. Frankfurt a. M.: Campus, 13-26.

Zolotas, X., 1981. Economic Growth and Declining Social Welfare. New York: NYU Press.

Ewa Czerwińska-Schupp (ed.)

Values and Norms in the Age of Globalization

Frankfurt am Main, Berlin, Bern, Bruxelles, New York, Oxford, Wien, 2007.
571 pp., num. fig.
Dia-Logos. Edited by Tadeusz Buksiński and Piotr W. Juchacz. Vol. 9
ISBN 978-3-631-55171-4 · pb. € 69.–*

The authors of this book, scholars from Germany, Austria, the United States, Kirghizia andPoland, seek an answer to the challenges posed to social sciences by the globalization epoch. The challenges apply to such problems as the establishment of rights and rules and institutions governing the existence of supra- and international communities, the development of a common system of ethical values, moral standards and norms (or even the creation of a system of entirely new values, standards and norms) supporting the unification process, as well as the legitimacy and validity of transferring the values and standards and the models of economy and politics characteristic of European culture to other cultures and civilizations. This book raises the questions that are particularly significant to the present-day political practice in its European and global dimensions: the questions of place, role and dimension, as well as topicality or transformations in the post-modern order of the world, of such moral values, standards and norms present in politics as human rights, freedom, justice, responsibility, solidarity, tolerance, forgiveness, peace, security, education, modernization or democracy and law.

Contents: Rights and Values in Philosophy · The European Community as a Community of Values · Values and Norms in Contemporary Societies · Science and Globalization Processes · Law Politics in the Context of the Challenges of Globalization · Democracy and Globalization

www.ingramcontent.com/pod-product-compliance
Ingram Content Group UK Ltd.
Pitfield, Milton Keynes, MK11 3LW, UK
UKHW021842100926
8556IPUK00019B/996

9 783631 570159